VOLUNTEER!

VOLUNTEER!

The Comprehensive Guide to Voluntary
Service in the U.S. and Abroad

1992-1993 edition

Edited by Max Terry

Council on International Educational Exchange
Council of Religious Volunteer Agencies

Volunteer! Copyright © 1992 by the Council on International Educational Exchange and the Council of Religious Volunteer Agencies. All rights reserved. Printed in the United States of America. No part of this book may be used or reproduced in any manner whatsoever without written permission except in the case of brief quotations embodied in critical articles or reviews. For information, contact CIEE, 205 East 42nd Street, New York, NY 10017.

Cover design by Amy King. Cover photo courtesy of City Volunteer Corps.

ISBN Number: 1-882036-12-3

1992–1993 edition.

CONTENTS

	PREFACE	vii
	ACKNOWLEDGMENTS	ix
Part I	**VOLUNTARY SERVICE: THE BASICS**	1
	Short-Term Projects	4
	International Workcamps	4
	Field Research Projects and Archaeological Digs	6
	Other Short-Term Opportunities	7
	Medium and Long-Term Placements	7
	Government Programs	8
	Religiously Affiliated Service	9
	Service-Learning	10
	Social Service Organizations	10
	Is Voluntary Service for You?	11
	Evaluating Programs	14
	How to Read the Listings	16
	Organizations Behind the Scenes	18
	Suggestions for Further Reading	20
Part II	**VOLUNTEER EXPERIENCES**	23
	Esperar: to wait, to hope by John Hathaway	26
	A Volunteer Vacation by Christopher Wright	29
	Volunteering with the Homeless by Lori McAdam	32
	Building Bridges by Nicole Ellison	35
Part III	**SHORT-TERM PROJECTS**	39
Part IV	**MEDIUM AND LONG-TERM PLACEMENTS**	101

APPENDIX 167
Council of Religious
    Volunteer Agencies (CRVA) 169
Council on International
    Educational Exchange (CIEE) 171

INDEX 179
Organizations and Publications 181
Skills Needed 185
Location of Programs 187

PREFACE

Welcome to the fourth edition of *Volunteer!* In these pages, you'll find a newly revised and encouragingly long list of voluntary service organizations which, through their work, make all our lives better and richer. We continue to be inspired by their dedication and this book is meant to encourage those of you who are thinking of volunteering and are still looking for where and how to best use your skills, time, and interests. Our purpose is to clarify the options available and to put you in touch with the people and organizations who most need you.

This book is a joint project of two organizations, the Council on International Educational Exchange (CIEE) and the Council of Religious Volunteer Agencies (CRVA). To anyone not familiar with these organizations, a few words of explanation.

The **Council on International Educational Exchange** is a private, nonprofit membership organization with offices in the U.S., Europe, and Asia. It was founded in 1947 to help reestablish student exchange after the Second World War. In its early years, CIEE chartered ocean liners for transatlantic student sailings, arranged group air travel, and organized orientation programs to prepare students and teachers for educational experiences abroad. Over the years, CIEE's mandate has broadened dramatically as the interests of its ever-increasing number of members have spread beyond Europe to Africa, Asia, and Latin America. Today, CIEE assumes a number of important responsibilities that include developing and administering programs of international educational exchange throughout the world, coordinating work-abroad programs and international workcamps, and facilitating inexpensive international travel for students, teachers, and other budget travelers. As part of its service to international travelers and to those who serve as their advisers, CIEE publishes *Work, Study, Travel Abroad: The Whole World Handbook*, presently in its eleventh edition, and *The Teenager's Guide to Study, Travel, and Adventure Abroad*. See the appendix for more information about CIEE.

The **Council of Religious Volunteer Agencies**, established in 1946 is a broad coalition of North American organizations (promoters, planners, users) of full-time voluntary service. With roots in the religious community, CRVA is an independent nonprofit association. Members include local community-based organizations using small numbers of volunteers and national agencies placing thousands of volunteers annually. Each year CRVA member organizations place over 100,000 full-time volunteers within the U.S. and around the world for periods of several weeks to three years. Through its biannual meetings, CRVA serves as a forum for sharing of ideas, programs, and resources among administrators of voluntary service organizations. In addition, CRVA also sponsors periodic consultations on topics of interest to the field of voluntary service. (CRVA and CIEE are full members of UNESCO's Coordinating Committee for International Voluntary Service.)

There are over 200 organizations listed in this edition. We've tried to screen the programs and choose only those we felt we could recommend, however, we cannot guarantee the quality of the programs. In the first chapter of this book, "Voluntary Service: The Basics" you'll find tips to help you evaluate programs for yourself.

We do not claim to have compiled an exhaustive list of opportunities. If you have additional information or any suggestions for the next edition, please let us know.

Acknowledgements

Many people deserve credit for helping to put together the latest edition of *Volunteer!* First and foremost, thanks to the publications staff at the Council on International Educational Exchange, especially Max Terry, the book's editor, who is also largely responsible for page layout and design. Lazaro Hernandez, who oversaw the project, also contributed much to both the content and the design of the finished book. Thanks also to Richard Christiano, Jon Howard, and Fraser Brown, who assisted in many phases of the book, including researching, proofreading, and indexing the manuscript.

Special gratitude needs to expressed to Carl Bade, Ed Doty, Janet Shrock, and Michael Stuart and the other members of the Council on Religious Volunteer Agencies for their help in reviewing the manuscript. The Council on Religious Volunteer Agencies provided much useful information and valuable feedback.

Recognition should also be given to Gina Chase, director of CIEE's voluntary service program, for her contribution to Part One of this book and her cooperation in providing photos and other materials used in this book.

In addition, thanks to all of the organizations described in this book for the information, photos, and quotes they provided. A special thanks to the City Volunteer Corps for providing the photo used on the cover of this book.

All of these people were part of the lengthy and sometimes tedious process of producing this book. Our efforts are more than rewarded, however, by the belief that the finished product will be of use in encouraging and informing individuals considering work in service of humanity.

Del Franz
Director, Information and Student Services
Council on International Educational Exchange

PART ONE
Voluntary Service: The Basics

VOLUNTARY SERVICE: THE BASICS

Voluntary service encompasses a wide range of activities, from putting in a few hours a week at a local homeless shelter to spending two weeks during the summer at a workcamp to devoting several years to teach in an African village. The one thing that ties them together is that they're all performed by people who want to experience the rewards of serving others. And the rewards are indeed great. A volunteer experience will give you the satisfaction of enriching the lives of other human beings, contribute to your personal growth, and broaden your knowledge of the world.

For the purposes of this book, we have limited our focus to those programs in need of full-time volunteers. To be a full-time volunteer means donating a solid chunk of time to your project, something like a nine to five commitment for anywhere from a weekend to several years. In many cases, being a full-time volunteer means leaving your home for the duration of your service, living in close quarters with other volunteers, and sometimes becoming immersed in a community that's culturally quite different from your own. In any case, volunteering full-time will probably present you with a radical change of lifestyle.

The vast number of full-time volunteer programs practically guarantees that one is right for you, whether you're a retired medical doctor wanting to share your experience in the Third World, a lawyer looking for a fulfilling way to spend your two-week vacation, or a recent college graduate seeking a foreign assignment while you decide your purpose in life. Next to the nature of the work itself, the length of time you want to commit may be the biggest factor in deciding which project is right for you. Keeping this in mind, we've organized our program listings into two categories: Short-Term Projects and Medium/Long-Term Placements. Below, we describe in further detail the different options available in each category. Remember, though, that these are broad, general categories intended to give some order to a wide range of possibilities.

Short-Term Projects

Short-term projects, sometimes known as "volunteer vacations," are geared to people with a limited amount of time to spare, usually lasting two to four weeks but sometimes up to two or three months. While a few projects recruit highly-skilled professionals (such as medical personnel), the vast majority require no previous experience. Most often, short-term volunteer projects become intense learning experiences. Some of the most popular forms of short-term service are workcamps, archaeological digs, and field research projects.

International Workcamps

Workcamps bring together 10 to 20 volunteers from perhaps as many countries to work on service projects around the world. Projects last two to four weeks, usually during the summer, and may include such tasks as construction of houses or schools in underprivileged communities, renovation of historic buildings or monuments, or preservation of parklands and other natural resources. Beyond the services workcamps provide, it's their international makeup that gives them their unique character.

There's simply no other way to develop close, working relationships with so many different people in so short a time. Volunteers not only work but live together in a communal environment. They collectively decide how to divide their labor on the project; how to share the cooking, cleaning, and other chores of daily life; and how to spend their leisure time together. The group, however, is not a self-contained unit. Each workcamp develops a special relationship with the surrounding community it serves and must remain sensitive to that community's needs. Above all, workcamp participants must be easygoing, flexible, and able to get along with others.

The first workcamp was organized in France in the aftermath of World War I by a Swiss pacifist named Pierre Ceresole and a British Quaker named Hubert Parris. They believed they could encourage international peace by bringing together young people from across the continent to repair the damage inflicted by Europe's most devastating war. It was not only destroyed houses and roads these volunteers were trying to rebuild; they were seeking to restore the personal ties between nations.

Workcamps have since grown into a worldwide movement sponsored primarily by a small number of national organizations. These national organizations identify community needs in their own countries, meet to share information on possible projects, and work together to recruit volunteers. Each organization receives volunteers to work locally in addition to sending local volunteers abroad. In the U.S., the three main national workcamp organizations are CIEE, Service Civil International (SCI), and Volunteers for Peace (VFP). Many foreign workcamp organizations require U.S. volunteers to apply through these three. In the short-term projects section of this book, we have indicated which foreign workcamps can be contacted directly and which must be contacted through a U.S. organization.

CIEE workcamp participants in La Roche sur Grane, France, helping to renovate the path to a 15th-century hamlet.

Churches and other religious organizations also organize a large variety of workcamps. While individual churches operate locally, many also cooperate with their national denominational organizations to send their members on workcamps throughout the country and sometimes around the world. Most do not require volunteers to belong to any particular religious group.

No matter who organizes the workcamp, however, conditions for participation are usually similar. Volunteers are expected to pay their own travel costs to and from the workcamp as well as a nominal administration fee. Room and board and all other work-related necessities are generally provided by the workcamp's host organization or by local communities.

Field Research Projects and Archaeological Digs

Every year, hundreds of scholars and scientists—botanists, zoologists, archaeologists—take to the field to gather information about our world. Many are accompanied by both skilled and unskilled assistants. This is where you come in.

Field research projects can last from a weekend to several months and take place in a wide variety of geographic locations. Activities range from whale-spotting off Alaska's Puget Sound to studying the ecological balance of the Javanese rain forest. A number of organizations, such as Earthwatch and the Foundation for Field Research, publish listings of upcoming expeditions in need of volunteer assistance. Since most research projects are undertaken privately, with the aid of university or foundation grants, they often ask volunteers to pay a fee to cover not only their own traveling and living expenses but also a share of the project's overall cost. These fees vary widely according to project type and location and they're usually tax-deductible as charitable contributions.

Foundation for Field Research volunteers recording native rock art in Grenada.

For those interested specifically in archaeological projects, a number of organizations can provide a wealth of information. The Archaeological Institute of America, a nonprofit organization chartered through the Smithsonian Institution, is the oldest archaeological organization in the U.S., founded in 1879. Its *Archaeological Fieldwork Opportunities Bulletin* ($12.50 for nonmembers), lists projects around the world in need of volunteers. You can write the Institute at 675 Commonwealth Avenue, Boston, MA 02215. Another good source of information is Archaeology Abroad (31-34 Gordon Square, London WC1H OPY, England) which publishes three bulletins each year.

Participating in a scientific-research project or an archaeological dig can be especially appealing. Working as part of an international team, volunteers find themselves in unusual settings where the excitement of making some new discovery is always a possibility. Whether you're a student considering a career in the sciences or someone who's just plain curious, becoming a member of a field research project or an archaeological dig is an extraordinary opportunity to become engaged in an active learning experience.

Other Short-Term Opportunities

Workcamps and field research projects are two special kinds of volunteer opportunities. Of course, there are many other kinds of short-term service. As you look through the Short-Term Projects section of this book, you'll be surprised by the number of things you can do within the space of a few weeks. Summer camps and orphan homes, facilities for the disabled and the aged—many would value your short-term commitment. There are opportunities for doctors to share their skills abroad, opportunities for students to show their support for the peoples of Central America, and opportunities to experience life in shelters for the homeless and refugees right here in the U.S. Just name the activity; you'll probably find an organization that needs your help.

Medium/Long-Term Placements

This category is especially broad, encompassing voluntary service assignments that range in time from three months to several years or even a lifetime. Often, the length of commitment is related to the amount of training and preparation required for service, as well as the ease with which various organizations can fill empty positions. In the U.S., for example, you'll run across a number of projects lasting a year or less; many overseas assignments, however, which require cultural orientation and language training, ask for a two- to three-year commitment.

Because of the amount of time involved, most organizations offering long-term positions do not expect their volunteers to shoulder all of their expenses. Many cover their volunteers' travel expenses and room and board, as well as providing a reasonable monthly stipend to cover personal costs. A few even provide returnees with a readjustment allowance to assist them with reestablishing themselves back home.

As you might imagine, a commitment of a year or more is a big decision to make, one that calls for plenty of serious thought. Long-term service creates a very definite break from most people's everyday lives, requiring more preparation before beginning and more readjustment upon completing the project. Long-term volunteers must establish themselves as a more integral part of the communities they serve and also have to bear more responsibility to the organizations they represent. Keeping these things in mind, it's very important to choose your program carefully. Below we describe some prevalent types of long-term service organizations.

Government Programs

Many countries' governments operate volunteer agencies to provide assistance to people suffering from widespread poverty, sickness, and natural disaster. The United States is no exception. ACTION is the federal government's umbrella organization for voluntary service. Under its direction, Volunteers in Service to America (VISTA) recruits people to work full-time with state and local agencies serving low-income communities throughout the country. VISTA volunteers live and work among this country's poor, in both urban and rural areas.

The U.S. agency that sends volunteers abroad is the Peace Corps, founded in 1961 by an executive order of President John F. Kennedy. For many, the Peace Corps has come to typify the idea of development assistance in the Third World. However, applicants should be aware that, as an agency of the U.S. Government, it is subject to government interests and policies.

As it celebrates its thirtieth anniversary, the Peace Corps continues to expand, initiating its first programs ever in Eastern Europe. It is also in the process of redefining its image, seeking to increase participation by ethnic minorities to better represent the racial and cultural makeup of the U.S. Although the Peace Corps recruits technical experts, it has traditionally reserved positions for "generalists" who don't necessarily have any experience beyond a college education.

One of many alternatives to the Peace Corps is the United Nations Volunteer Program, which also provides technical assistance and training to developing countries around the world.

Although the Peace Corps processes all U.S. applicants for UN Volunteers, there are many differences between the two. UN Volunteers operates under the auspices of the United Nations, recruiting participants from many different countries, both developed and developing. Participants from the U.S. make up only a small percentage of the total. And unlike the Peace Corps, UN Volunteers recruits only experienced personnel, either those who have volunteered overseas before or who have several years of useful work experience.

Religiously Affiliated Service

A great number of voluntary service organizations are affiliated with churches or other religious groups. Some of these organizations are directly governed by specific churches and require participants to be practicing members; most, however, are simply inspired by religious ideals which they do not attempt to impose upon either their participants or those they serve. If you're imagining the kind of missionary activity that went on during the heyday of European colonialism, you'll be surprised to discover the more varied and practical nature of many of these service programs. Some send volunteers abroad in the capacity of relief workers, teachers, and technical advisers. Others do their work here in the U.S. at homeless shelters, hospitals, and centers for Central American refugees. Of course, the religiously-rooted volunteer movement encompasses a broad variety of faiths as well as political orientations; each program should be considered individually. Whether you're deeply religious or not, you might find an excellent volunteer opportunity through one of these organizations.

Association of Episcopal Colleges volunteer clearing a field for a children's playground in Appalachia.

Service-Learning

It should come as no surprise that most volunteers learn a great deal from their experiences. The recognition of this fact has led to a new concept in education called service-learning, an option open to university students which links structured learning and voluntary service for academic credit.

A number of colleges and universities have begun to adopt programs in which students spend a summer, semester, or year working in orphanages in Mexico or teaching English in the Philippines, just to name two examples. While performing their service, they study subjects ranging from history and language to the sciences. At schools where this type of program doesn't exist, many students have created their own service-learning programs as a kind of independent study project.

One of the leaders in the service-learning field is the Partnership for Service-Learning, which works with a number of institutions to establish service-learning projects in the U.S. and abroad. The Partnership operates its own off-campus programs in which academic study is directed by the faculty of an in-country, four-year, accredited institution, which issues an official transcript for the studies. Students are also sponsored by a local service organization, which provides students with volunteer work in conjunction with their academic studies. Check to see if your college or university will let you pursue one of these options.

Social Service Organizations

There is a wide range of long-term programs offered by what may generally be described as social service organizations. These are private, nonprofit, nonsectarian organizations dedicated to improving the lives of others. The kinds of services they provide vary greatly. For example, volunteers can spend a year teaching abroad through organizations such as WorldTeach and the YMCA. Political refugees, in the U.S. and overseas, are assisted by volunteers working through the American Refugee Committee and the International Rescue Committee. Medical personnel of all specializations volunteer abroad through organizations like Health Volunteers Overseas, Dental Health International, and the International Eye Foundation. Volunteers for the Coalition for the Homeless and the International Fourth World Movement live with the poor and the homeless. These are just a few examples randomly selected from our listings. Many more await you!

Is Voluntary Service for You?

One of the things we've been trying to communicate in this introduction is that you don't need to be a doctor or an agronomist to make a capable volunteer. In addition, we've been attempting to point out that volunteering requires a special kind of person. Above all, volunteers need to maintain the proper attitude toward their work. This will often be the biggest challenge of all.

While people volunteer for many reasons, most volunteers share a certain amount of idealism. They want to make a difference in the world and they're willing to work without pay to do it. Instead, they expect to receive a sort of spiritual fulfillment from their labors, the kind of satisfaction that comes from helping others or from the successful completion of a difficult task. All this is perfectly reasonable; but it's important for volunteers to have more realistic expectations of what they can accomplish through their service and what they will return with in exchange.

For example, you may embark upon a one-year assignment as a famine relief worker in the Sudan. Despite your efforts to distribute food in local villages, shipments from outside the country are delayed for various reasons. You're tempted to give up out of frustration, but you have to keep working in the face of what seems an insurmountable problem. In the end, you realize that you could do nothing to change a terrible situation, that the only change occurred within yourself, and that it isn't very easy to figure out exactly what that change means.

Or, suppose you choose to spend a few weeks on an archaeological dig in northern New Mexico searching for an ancient Pueblo village. You've really been looking forward to this dig, imagining your delight upon unearthing that first clay vessel. As it turns out, nobody finds a thing; you spend day after day in the hot desert sun sifting gravel through screens, and all you have to show for your trouble are an aching back and sun-blistered neck. It certainly wasn't what you expected, but

12 Volunteer!

you did learn a lot about what archaeologists go through on a bad day!

Of course, both of these examples are overly simplified. In spite of frustrations, a year of relief work in Africa may well be the greatest adventure you have ever faced. And though you might search in vain for that buried village, you may very well meet some fascinating people on the dig. Often the rewards of volunteering come from unexpected sources. For this reason it's important to rid yourself of rigid preconceptions and to go into your experience with an open mind.

In the box at left, you'll find a few questions to help you decide if a voluntary service commitment is right for you. While these questions may seem abstract, they do point to qualities and attitudes that help a volunteer work successfully. If you have difficulty imagining the kind of situation in which these qualities would come in handy, read through the following examples of what happened to a few volunteers and try to imagine if you would have reacted differently.

> **Questions You Should Ask Yourself:**
>
> - Are you flexible?
> - Can you function independently?
> - Are you willing to serve others in the way they want to be served?
> - Are you capable of showing initiative?
> - Can you cope with total involvement in the community you serve?
> - Do you have a sense of humor?
> - Are you willing to critically assess your own beliefs and views?
> - Can you cope with being away from friends and family?
> - Can you accept cultural differences?
> - Can you live and work as a member of a team?

Dealing with expectations:

When I arrived in Istanbul for the orientation I found the program and the participants not to be what or who I expected from the brief description I initially received. Furthermore, the village to which we were assigned had not received the materials for the work we were to do! They were going to "find" a task for us to do. I was concerned that such a task would not really be needed by the people of the village, and only a way to occupy our time. After speaking to the director, I chose not to stay.

It's very difficult to readjust your expectations right on the spot but the need to do so occurs often in voluntary service. Organizations who are used to accomplishing their mission through donations of materials, money, and other people's time, deal everyday with unmet deadlines, slower timetables, and the frustration that goes with it. Can you?

Adjusting to different attitudes:
In my workcamp I experienced different forms of sexism than what I was used to. Having so many females on this project and a couple of really sexist men from Algeria, we were in constant friction, just not understanding each other. I'll never forget the first day when one of them walked in, sat down, looked at us females questioningly and demanded, "coffee." It calmed down a little at the end of the project but we mainly learned to grin and bear it (them, too!) rather than solving anything. I think I learned that when two people have completely different views that they grow up with, just hearing another's views won't change anything. We thought they were being stubborn for not seeing the right choice; they thought we were wrong.

Sexism, racism, prejudices of all shapes and colors, are not so easy to identify in ourselves. On a broader level they are part of the many preconceptions that we carry with us. We often take for granted that what we do is right and therefore, whatever is different must be wrong. Being able to understand where you come from and to live with differences is a great test. How would you pass it?

Understanding the effect you have on others:
One day, when I was just starting into my morning work, all the village children gathered around me. I realized then that they were pointing at my Walkman headphones. They'd never seen such things before, so I let them listen. Big mistake! From then on, the children had full control of my Walkman and all my tapes. But I figured, "What the heck!"

If you volunteer in areas where the people aren't accustomed to consumer-oriented technological gadgetry, you can expect them to be curious about any unusual possessions you might have. This person probably didn't think anything about bringing her Walkman along, and thus could not anticipate the excitement such an object could inspire. It's always wise to be critically aware of the baggage you take with you—whether it's material possessions or cultural attitudes. Of course, nobody can be completely aware of the image they project. The best solution is to do as this woman did: relax and go with the flow.

While many of the qualities needed in a volunteer may seem innate to certain people, most can be developed with a little effort. If you want to have a good volunteer experience, you have to prepare yourself as thoroughly as you can.

If you're going to another country, you should learn about the culture, history, and politics of the people among whom you'll be living. Most long-term programs require that applicants speak the language of the host-country, or that they undergo training before their service. Even if fluency is not a requirement, it's a good idea to familiarize yourself with the language; after all, communication is key. One of the best ways to prepare yourself is to make personal contact with someone from that country. A few hours of conversation can teach you more than several books.

It's also a good idea to learn as much as possible about the organization sponsoring your project, whether you're going abroad or staying in the U.S. You should request all the information they have (brochures, annual reports, newsletters) and read it carefully. If possible, try to meet former participants. Most voluntary service organizations will be happy to give you the names and addresses of people you can contact. In this way, you can develop some idea of what to expect from your project.

Evaluating Programs

One of the more difficult challenges, of course, is finding the project that's right for you. In compiling our list of voluntary service programs, we've given you several leads; it's up to you to take the next step and follow through. As you further investigate volunteer opportunities, you may run across programs not listed in this edition. Whether the program you're interested in is in this book or not, here are some questions which will help you to evaluate it:

1. Who is the sponsoring organization? What is its affiliation? Although many of the programs you'll come across

Voluntary Service: The Basics 15

may not sound familiar, they may be affiliated with larger entities. Be sure to find out exactly who you'll be serving.

2. What is the financial situation of the sponsoring organization? Is it tax exempt? How does it finance itself? What role, if any, will you be expected to play in its fund-raising activities? Remember that you can always ask for the organization's annual report in order to get an accurate account of its finances.

3. What do former volunteers have to say about the program? Any worthwhile organization is willing to give the names of former participants so that you can contact them yourself and ask for a first-hand report on their experiences. The value of this kind of contact cannot be overemphasized.

4. What kind of provision will be made for health insurance while you are in service? Some programs provide insurance, others require participants to provide their own. Either situation is acceptable, but be sure to know which applies.

5. What kind of staff supervision is provided in conjunction with the program? This varies enormously among programs and, like the insurance question above, it is something that should be clearly spelled out before you begin service.

6. If you have a student loan, is it possible to have payments deferred while you are in service? According to Public Law 96-374, 3ACFR, Part 682-508 of the Guaranteed Student Loan Program, borrowers serving as volunteers in programs which meet specific requirements may have their payments deferred for the time of service.

7. What are the living arrangements going to be? Obviously, you can't expect luxury, but it's best to be prepared for whatever's coming. Ask the organization to be specific about the range of possible accommodations. Here too, former participants will be enormously helpful.

8. What happens if you can't complete your term of service? Although we hope it won't happen, it can. You should know how the organization will react.

9. How does the organization prepare its participants for their experience? Carefully review any orientation material or plans and look at any written material with a

16 Volunteer!

critical eye. Trust your instincts on these things; you have to feel absolutely confident about your choice of sponsoring organization before you begin service.

10. If the position is overseas, what are the necessary visas or other official papers that you'll need and how are they to be obtained? What about health regulations—any necessary vaccinations or other precautions for the part of the world you're going to?

How to Read the Listings

As noted before, we've arranged the listings into two major sections: Short-Term Projects and Medium/Long-Term Placements. Within each category, organizations are listed alphabetically. If you don't have any particular organization in mind, but you do have some idea of what you want to do or where you want to go, you should refer to the index at the back of the book. Besides the general index, we've included an index of skills needed and an index of locations (by continent and country).

These listings are intended to give you an overall feel for each organization. We've tried to go beyond listing just the basic facts, providing as much general description as we could in this limited space. We've also included photographs of project activities and quotations from former volunteers whenever possible. Within each listing, after the organization's address and telephone number, you'll find the following items:

Organization: This describes, in broad terms, what the sponsoring group is all about; it usually includes a short history of the organization and a statement of general purpose.

Program: This describes the actual voluntary service positions which the organization sponsors, the specific time commitment (if any), the nature of the assignment, the location and, where applicable, information on orientation procedures.

Requirements: Here are listed any skills, languages, or degrees required. Where sponsors give us a list of less concrete qualities they're looking for—things like maturity, sense of humor, reliability—we mention them here.

Age: If there's a minimum or maximum age requirement, it is noted here.

Living Arrangements: We ask sponsors to describe the conditions in which their volunteers live. This information is meant to give you an insight into the atmosphere of the service environment.

Persons with Disabilities: This category lists the policy of the organization regarding participation by persons with disabilities. Where applicable, we note any special facilities that persons with disabilities may have at their disposal.

Finances: This is where we talk about expenses. It may describe what the sponsor provides, including room, board, a stipend, a travel allowance, or any combination of the above. In some cases, the sponsor doesn't provide anything at all, relying on the volunteer to be entirely self-sufficient. Volunteers must pay to participate in some of the programs. In these cases, we've noted the fee and, wherever possible, specified what it covers. Programs for which volunteers are asked to do fund raising are also noted.

Deadline: Some programs have specific deadlines, others none at all. We've noted either case.

Contact: In order to be sure your inquiry goes to the right person, we've given a name and a title to contact. In some of the smaller agencies, the name of the contact is not important, but in the larger organizations, taking care to use them will help prevent your written request from getting lost in a pile of mail or your telephone call from being put on hold for an afternoon. Beware, there may be changes in the organization at any time so that the person listed here may not still be behind the same desk. Even then, having a name to ask for should help get your request to the right person.

The first step in applying to any voluntary service program is to send an inquiry letter, including either a separate resume or a paragraph or two about yourself—your age, education, work experience, interests, etc. This will help the placement organization determine whether or not you're suitable for a position. If you're corresponding with an organization overseas, send an international postal reply coupon, available at any post office, to cover their postage costs.

Organizations Behind the Scenes

The organizations listed in this book either have their own volunteer programs or serve as matchmakers, putting prospective volunteers in touch with appropriate programs. In addition, there are other organizations, not involved with placement, which are active behind the scenes of voluntary service, providing information and other services. Because these behind-the-scenes organizations cooperate with many others, they are in a good position to help you find specific programs.

One such organization is **InterAction**, located at 1717 Massachusetts Avenue NW, Eighth Floor, Washington, DC 20036. InterAction, the result of a merger between the American Council of Voluntary Agencies for Foreign Service and Private Agencies in International Development (PAID), has over 130 members—all nonprofit organizations engaged in development work. Two of InterActions' publications are *Member Profiles* ($25, plus $3 postage) which describes its members' activities and *Diversity in Development* ($30, plus $3 postage) which describes member programs in Africa.

The Human Environment Center (HEC), located at 1001 Connecticut Avenue NW, Suite 827, Washington, DC 20036, helps to coordinate the efforts of various environmental and social justice organizations and operates a recruitment and placement program for careers in the environmental field. HEC also houses the **National Association of Service and Conservation Corps (NASCC)**, which serves youth corps programs as a national clearinghouse and information exchange network, and provides technical assistance and training to strengthen and expand new and existing youth corps programs. A one year subscription to its quarterly newsletter, *Youth Can!*, costs $25.

Another important organization promoting community service among college students is the **Campus Outreach Opportunity League (COOL)**. COOL's national network includes over 400 campuses and 150 national, state, and local organizations. It offers consulting services, publications (including a manual on how to start up and run a campus community service organization), meetings, and special projects. For information, contact COOL at 386 McNeal Hall, University of Minnesota, St. Paul, MN 55108.

The American Red Cross is a humanitarian organization, led by volunteers, that provides relief to victims of disasters and helps people prevent, prepare for, and respond to emergencies. It does this through services that are consistent with its Congressional charter and the fundamental principles of the International Red Cross Movement. Over one million volunteers serve in management, advisory, and direct-service capacities. Representative areas of volunteer service include disaster preparedness and response, blood collection assistance, health and safety courses, AIDS education, youth development, and military/social services. Opportunities exist for both full- and part-time volunteer involvement, including selected international opportunities. Because the Red Cross is largely community-based and very widespread, you should contact your local branch for more information.

Perhaps the best known source of information on voluntary service programs in general and workcamps in particular is the **Coordinating Committee for International Voluntary Service (CCIVS)**, UNESCO, 1, rue Miollis, 75015 Paris, France. CCIVS represents 125 organizations who are involved in long-, medium-, or short-term voluntary service. It assists UNESCO (the United Nations' Educational, Scientific, and Cultural Organization) in the implementation of programs relating to both educational growth and international development. Each year, the Committee publishes its *Workcamps Programme List* which gives the addresses of organizations in over 50 countries, many of which are described in this book. Copies may be ordered from Paris (four international reply coupons should be enclosed with all requests) but be sure to contact a workcamp organization in your own country first, because most of the organizations listed in the CCIVS program will not accept an individual whose application is not forwarded by a cooperating workcamp organization.

Suggestions for Further Reading

Listed below are a few books that could be helpful as you prepare for your voluntary service assignment. As you will see, some of these publications address issues of going overseas. However, because voluntary service, even in the U.S., often involves working in different cultural settings, many of the qualities which make an overseas experience successful are also prerequisites for voluntary service, whether at home or abroad. Thus, these books should make good reading for anyone about to volunteer.

Survival Kit for Overseas Living (second edition, 1984) by L. Robert Kohls, published by Intercultural Press, P.O. Box 700, Yarmouth, ME 04096 ($7.95 plus $2 book-rate postage) is good mental preparation for Americans planning to live and work abroad. Kohls' thesis is that what people need most when they go abroad is to understand their own "cultural baggage" so that they can "avoid tripping over it too often." With this in mind, he takes the reader through those aspects of living overseas which most often create problems for the unwary traveler. Intercultural Press carries a full line of books dealing with cross-cultural issues, including many country-specific titles. Another excellent, more recent title is *The Art of Crossing Cultures* ($14.95), by Craig Storti, which examines the basic psychological processes involved in confronting a foreign culture, making use of numerous literary works to illustrate his model.

Trans-Cultural Study Guide (1988) is published by Volunteers in Asia. Calling upon their first-hand experience with volunteers and their hosts, the compilers of the book believe that by systematically pursuing the answers to certain sets of questions, the traveler can acquire the knowledge needed to provide a solid base for understanding and working in another country. The hundreds of questions suggested by the authors are grouped under such headings as art, music, economics, food, social structure, etc. The *Guide* costs $4.95 and can be ordered by writing to Box 4543, Stanford, CA 94309. VIA also publishes other useful resources. The 1986 edition of its *Appropiate Technology Sourcebook* ($17.95), by Ken Darrow and Mike Saxenian, reviews 1150 of the best small-scale technology books from around the world. If you need how-to information on any development project from building a bridge to seeding a forest, this sourcebook will point you in the right direction. Health-conscious volunteers going abroad should read *Staying Healthy in Asia, Africa, and Latin America* ($7.50), by Dirk Schroeder, an excellent guide to first-aid and prevention. Add $1.50 postage for individual orders ($.50 extra for each additional book).

What You Can Do For Your Country, by Karen Schwartz, is the first comprehensive history of the Peace Corps. Published in 1991 by William Morrow and Company, this book not only provides a detailed and well-balanced account of the Peace Corps' origins and organizational history, but also gives former volunteers the chance to relate their own experiences first-hand. This thought-provoking text is a must-read for anyone interested in joining the Corps. If you can't find it in bookstores, order by mail for $23 (includes postage) from Trouper Books, Box 164, 61 East Eighth Street, New York, NY 10003.

Work, Study, Travel Abroad: The Whole World Handbook, compiled by CIEE, is a good reference for college students and other young people going overseas. Although you won't find any more information on voluntary service opportunities than you will here, the book includes all the other possibilities for international experience—study, work, and internships, in addition to the nitty-gritty of inexpensive travel and the how-to's of getting ready for an international experience. Organized by geographical region, the book covers 75 countries in detail. The 1992-93 edition is available in bookstores, at Council Travel offices, or by mail from CIEE, 205 East 42nd Street, New York, NY 10017 for $12.95 (plus $1.50 book-rate postage; $3 for first-class).

The Overseas List, by David M. Beckmann and Elizabeth Anne Donnelly is excellent reading for anyone interested in careers related to voluntary service abroad. Written for "idealistic young people, middle-aged Christians who find their jobs unfulfilling and retirees looking for a second career," it describes opportunities in the Third World, with the emphasis on service through career employment; it's meant to "offer guidelines in selecting an employer who is worth serving." Published by Bread for the World, it is available from Augsburg Publishing House, 426 South 5th Street, Minneapolis, MN 55440, for $12.95 plus $1.00 postage.

PART TWO
Volunteer Experiences

VOLUNTEER EXPERIENCES

To help you form a better idea as to what volunteering is all about, we've asked a number of former volunteers to contribute essays about their experiences. Volunteering is a personal commitment, a decision made by different people for many different reasons. But although each experience is unique, there's still no better way to get a feel for a voluntary service program, or of volunteering in general, than by listening to what past participants have to say.

You may already have a friend who has volunteered and would be happy to give you some advice. If you are interested in a particular program, you should ask the sponsoring organization to supply you with a list of participants you can contact. Whatever you do, be sure to talk to somebody.

The volunteers who contributed the following essays have served in a variety of ways, and each looks back on the experience from a different perspective. John Hathaway spent a semester in Ecuador with the Partnership for Service Learning, continuing his university studies while working for a community-based relief agency. Christopher Wright travelled to Jamaica with Global Volunteers for a brief but rewarding volunteer vacation. Lori McAdam learned a number of things about urban homelessness by working in a shelter in Berkeley, California. On a CIEE workcamp in Idaho, Nicole Ellison made new friends and learned a few woodsmen's tricks. Their essays are brief, and though they represent only part of the complete spectrum of volunteer activity we hope they will give you some idea of the opportunities that await you.

esperar: to wait, to hope

by John Hathaway

During my service assignment in Ecuador in an international agency serving the children and people of the community, I had one day which was indicative of my entire experience. My story is also in some ways representative of the good and bad points of the program in general. I hope, by starting with this story, my later points will be more clearly understood, and that my sometimes caustic criticisms of the agency will be taken with a grain of salt and an understanding of the community's need for the services they offer.

> **The feelings and help of gringos come second in this organization. I realize now that this is how it should be.**

My day started as usual. I arrived shortly after 8:30 a.m. and found a spot on an office counter to sit and try out my mediocre Spanish on the other workers, while I waited for my other gringo friends to arrive.

In a building roughly the size of a country-club swimming pool, there are, I would guess, over twenty-five people working full-time. These people would filter in as I sat on my linoleum perch and offer me friendly greetings. I would talk about my weekend or my classes, and whether I spoke in the first person or the second person it was invariably in the wrong person. But these people didn't seem to mind, and would always listen to me with genuine interest and helpful corrections.

When my friends arrived, we sat and waited together for someone to tell us to do something. Esperar: to wait, to hope. This is an important word to understand when trying to describe my agency—whether it was waiting for more paint to arrive at the worksite or waiting for someone to remember the gringos and tell us what to do or where to go. This day wasn't different. We waited and waited as people sifted in and out of the building.

I didn't figure out the rest of the story until after it happened, and I blame this on my Spanish, but it goes something like this. At a little after 10 a.m. the office received a call from a mother in a neighborhood a short distance away. She said that her child was sick and needed a ride to a nearby hospital. We were told by one of the many bosses in the office that there was a building needing painting near the house of the sick child, and therefore we were to accompany the driver to the neighborhood where we would be dropped off to paint. In all honesty, I was upset as we drove along. It was now close to 11:00, and because of our class schedules, we gringos had to leave work at noon. There had been too many days in the past three months where we had arrived at a job site with barely enough time to sweep the front porch or dip the brush into the paint can before we had to leave.

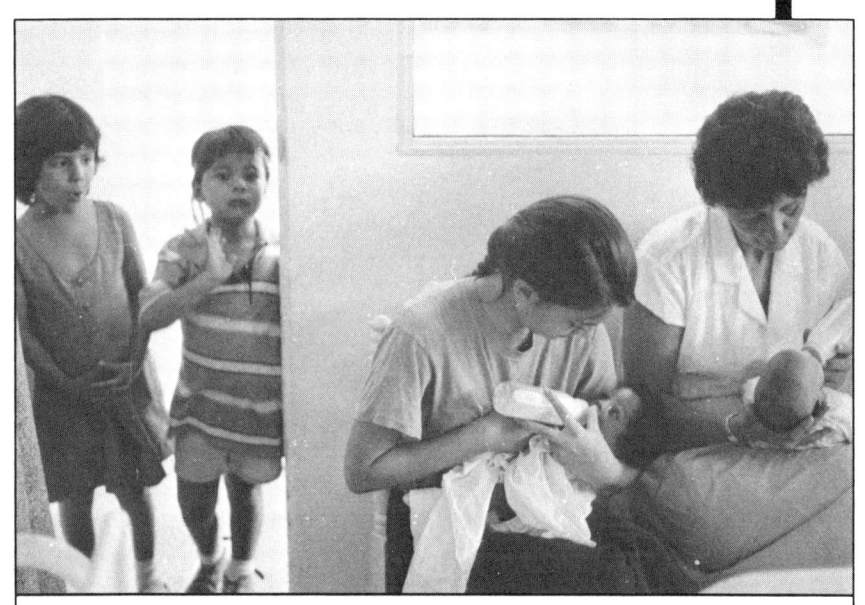

A volunteer with the Partnership for Service-Learning caring for children at an orphanage in Ecuador.

I was upset. Not talking much and taking huge, angry drags off my cigarette, I stared out the car window and watched the scenery speed by. I figured we would arrive at the job site about 11:15 and have only fifteen minutes to work before piling into the van again for the half hour ride back to the office.

We arrived at the job site and the driver leaned out the window to talk with an elderly, overweight woman dressed in a Disneyland T-shirt and a checkered skirt. After talking with her for five minutes, he leaned back and said that there was no paint. I took a drag off my cigarette and held the smoke in my lungs, hoping this would quell my anger, but it just made me cough. Without saying another word we sped to our other objective, the woman's house, to pick up the sick child.

We arrived at the woman's house and walked inside. The child lay perfectly still with a line of white film on his lips. Looking at the color of the child's skin we knew immediately that he was dead. The mother stood next to the child with a very, very blank look on her face. The driver, who was jovial and fairly unconcerned, took on the air of a man who had experienced this scene too many times before. He took the mother by her arm and led her to the van. The agency, he explained, would pay for the funeral and other expenses. The mother had only to sign some papers.

The ride back to the office was silent and powerful. The mother cried silently with her hands over her eyes. The guilt I felt was immense. Here was a mother who had just lost her child, and all that I was worried about was getting back on time for my classes.

This is the end of my story. The agency is an institution with many faults. A lack of administrative organization causes a great deal of confusion at times. Many times my friends and I felt that we were not really needed.

There is, however, a different side to the organization. Although the agency seemed to me, as a gringo, very disorganized, it serves an important and necessary function. There are so many poor people in Guayaquil who cannot possibly earn a living for their entire family. The agency provides rice and sugar for them as well as bright coloured dresses and toys for their children, and when there is a death, the agency provides a dignified funeral.

The feelings and help of gringos come second in this organization. I realize now that this is how it should be. If there is no work to satisfy my social conscience; if I have to wait for hours in the office; if there is no paint at the job site—so what! The fact is that this agency, through world-wide sponsorship, provides services that do help the people of the community. This simple fact makes the administrative problems (and the irritable nature of the gringos) seem unimportant and trivial.

A Volunteer Vacation

by Christopher Wright

Like many people, I have occasionally dreamt of chucking it all and joining the Peace Corps. But, like most people, I wasn't sure I wanted to spend two years overseas. I wanted to explore the world, but not as a tourist. So one spring, I decided to investigate short-term volunteer opportunities overseas. I came across a brochure for Global Volunteers, an organization based in St. Paul, Minnesota that sends short-term volunteer teams to villages in eight countries around the world to help rural people develop their communities. At the same time, the nonprofit, nonsectarian organization provides volunteers with an opportunity to gain a genuine, first-hand understanding of how rural people live day-to-day. True, I had to pay my own way, but no specific skills or technical expertise were required, and no religious beliefs were necessary. I liked that, so I signed up.

The project I chose was with a two-week team going to Jamaica to work in Woburn Lawn, a village 3000 feet up in the famous coffee-producing Blue Mountains. Woburn Lawn has a population of about 400 people, mostly small farmers. The community is strung along a winding road that's little better than a wide donkey path; it was washed out by Hurricane Gilbert in 1988. Gilbert caused great damage to the whole island, and the region around Woburn Lawn in particular.

The local economy is dependent on coffee. Farmers don't get a very good price for their crop due to international treaties and local and international monopolies. But recently, a few farmers have started branching out into other specialty crops. Carlton, a respected young village leader and entrepreneurial farmer, has had some success with a certain type of pepper. He is one of a few highly motivated risk-takers who are striving to bring about change themselves rather than wait for it to be given to them. This spirit is growing among the rural people, though many basic needs—transportation, access to education, and health care—remain underdeveloped.

30 Volunteer!

Our team worked alongside local volunteers on a number of projects. Rinna, a retired school teacher, worked in the local school with both students and teachers. Colleen, a biochemist, went to the preschool to work with the teachers there, Patricia and Doralynn. Pat, a nurse, made house calls and worked in the library with two young local people, Nicky and Duke. This library, which needed the rest of its books catalogued, was started with Global Volunteers' assistance and boxes of donated books. Our team leader Patricia and I worked with village men under the supervision of Mr. Charington, the master mason. Our project was the continuation of a cement block wall around the preschool yard, built to keep animals out of the playground and to keep children in.

Christopher Wright and a Jamaican volunteer cut wood to construct a wall in the village of Woburn Lawn.

Throughout the first week, work went smoothly and we became more and more familiar with our friends. We met a lot of people as we walked and worked around town, and started feeling more relaxed as Woburn Lawn began to feel like home. In the evenings we went up to the square for beer and Reggae dancing, and met people who, unable to take time away from their jobs to work with us, were happy to talk with us. One young coffee factory worker, nicknamed Duck, gave us lessons on the proper way to dance to the loping rhythm of Reggae.

Time passed quickly. Work on the wall went so well that we managed to build one more section than originally planned. The library organizing was finished in preparation for a visit from the Jamaica Library Exchange, which was expected to bring Woburn Lawn into its system. Pat continued making rounds, although she was unable to do more than wash and bandage sores and scratches, wash out eyes, take blood pressure—which is universally high—and dispense advice. But the interest she took in the villagers' health still made a positive impact.

Rinna found fertile ground in the school. She was able to give the teachers some creative ideas for supplementing the limited supplies of books and pencils and paper. Colleen made an impact in the preschool. While helping to teach, she

> Looking back, the only tangible evidence of our having been in Woburn Lawn was the addition of about 30 feet to a wall...But it's not the tangibles that are of the greatest importance.

also involved Tony, an aspiring artist, and Jordene, a young woman with a beautiful singing voice. Tony drew colorful illustrations to hang on the wall as visual aids, and Jordene came in to entertain and teach the children songs.

During our last day in the village, we met with Annabelle, the village matriarch. Annabelle is well into her seventies, sits on the board of the local Co-op, is president of the Woburn Lawn Women's Group, and continues to work in her fields growing and harvesting coffee beans and other crops. She speaks and writes in the language of the Bible, and has the respect of the village because of her love and concern for everyone and everything in it, including us; she gave us each a pound of coffee as thanks for our work.

As the team prepared to leave the village, we realized how our perceptions had changed. We had arrived thinking we would help these people by giving them creative ideas with which to develop their economy. But what we learned was that the people of Woburn Lawn have no shortage of ideas. They are resourceful and creative people. Looking back, the only tangible evidence of our having been in Woburn Lawn was the addition of about 30 feet to a wall, and a slightly better organized library. But it's not the tangibles that are of the greatest importance, it's the intangibles: the friendship, respect, and understanding that comes from working with other people. And all this in just two weeks.

Volunteering with the Homeless

by Lori McAdam

Two years ago, I was a delegate to the UCC General Synod (the national policy-making body of the United Church of Christ) in Fort Worth, Texas. During the Synod, it was voted that homelessness was to be the number one priority of the UCC. During the conference, there was a terrible, tornado-like storm from which a homeless man sought shelter in the convention center. I watched as he was ignored and shunned by the ministers and lay persons around him. The hypocrisy of this situation made a deep impression on me.

During the Synod, I also found out about the UCC's volunteer opportunities. The Summer Bridge program in Berkeley, California, stood out in my mind since it dealt with homelessness, and I was now curious about issues related to homelessness. Though there are many homeless people in Montana, my home state, the problem is not as visible as in other more urbanized areas of the country.

> Due to the diversity within this particular homeless community, there is no "one perfect solution" to their problems.

The Summer Bridge program integrates college students into the Berkeley Ecumenical Chaplaincy to the Homeless (BECH). BECH is sponsored by 14 Berkeley congregations and is funded primarily by donations. Homeless and formerly homeless people are trained to be peer chaplains who actively participate in programming for the organization and network in the homeless community. In this way, BECH utilizes the talents of homeless in order to address concerns of the homeless community through programs such as street counseling, cottage industries, community organizing, newsletter production, inspirational Bible studies and services, and transitional housing.

When I first arrived in Berkeley, I was completely overwhelmed by all of the people and activity. I had no idea what the project would be like, and I was quite sure I would not be able to handle it the first time I walked down Telegraph Avenue.

During the six-week period, I spent time getting to know several people in People's Park, as well as on Telegraph Avenue, and at the Oregon Street Drop-In Center. Homeless people live in this park and hang out along the avenue. The Oregon Street Drop-In is primarily frequented by mentally ill black men. At first, I felt very uncomfortable there. Despite this discomfort, two of my most meaningful friendships developed in that setting. My conversations with these people helped dispel a number of myths about the homeless community. I learned, for example, that drugs do not necessarily lead people into homelessness. Often, drug use is an attempt for homeless people to distance themselves from the harsh realities of daily life.

Lori McAdam (second from left) with fellow Summer Bridge volunteers in Berkeley, California.

While reflecting on my experiences in Berkeley, there are two main points that keep reappearing in my mind. First, the homeless are a very diverse group. There are drug users, alcoholics, and criminals; but there are also many who do not use drugs and many honest people. In this regard, the homeless community reflects society at large. I also realized that homeless people have a wide range of backgrounds and talents. Many, surprisingly, were not from the Berkeley area. It seems that homeless people from many states with inadequate social services come to Berkeley with hopes of finding a way to satisfy their basic needs. Due to the diversity within this particular homeless community, there is no "one perfect solution" to their problems.

Second, I became aware that many homeless people have incredible faith in God. When I first began to hear people's stories, I thought, "How can these people have faith in God after He has allowed such tragic things to happen in their lives?" Often, people confided to me that their strong faith is what gives them strength to continue living from day to day. I had never before witnessed the intense faith which I saw in the homeless community. There are Christian qualities about the lifestyle of most of the homeless people with whom I was involved. Food and clothes are shared and exchanged freely, and outsiders were welcomed into the group.

The structure of Summer Bridge lent itself to personal growth. Thanks to the Summer Bridge program, I became a part of a unique group of young women. I felt as though I've known these women much longer than the six weeks we spent together. Our shared experiences created a strong bond between us that remains special to me. There was a supportive atmosphere in our group that enabled both personal and spiritual concerns to be addressed. I was deeply moved by our discussions about religion and spirituality. Never before had I been a part of a group where each of its members were so respectful of individual differences and able to share so honestly without fear of judgement.

My decision to participate in Summer Bridge was my response to a deep sense that there was something missing in my life spiritually. I found that something in the chaplaincy. I found spiritual inspiration and the motivation to seek new ways to develop my own sense of spirituality. I found a safe place to share with my peers my hope to eventually go to seminary. I found compassion and love in places I never would have searched before. Most of all, I found hope. The chaplaincy inspires hope in the homeless community. And now, I have new hope that I will be able to respond to my calling from God.

Building Bridges

by Nicole Ellison

It was dark by the time the bus dropped me off at Bonner's Ferry, Idaho—and much quieter than Los Angeles, where I'd boarded a plane twelve hours earlier. Actually, Bonner's isn't big enough to warrant a bus station. We arrived at the local gas station, conveniently located between the Chick 'n' Chop Restaurant and the Russ Teek Inn. This was when I first realized that I was in for a very interesting three weeks.

I had originally signed up for the workcamp when I was living in New York City, but deciding that I couldn't bear another east coast winter, I moved out to Los Angeles, almost forgetting about my commitment during all the commotion. By the time the workcamp began, I had barely settled into my new place and was still looking for a job. I spent a day debating whether or not it was wise for me to take off in the middle of this rather hectic period in my life, but deciding that perhaps the fresh air would clear my head, I made trails for Idaho's northernmost reaches. The fact that I emerged not only with my sanity intact but also with the feeling that this was one of the best decisions I'd ever made is a testament to the setup of the camp and to the wonderful people participating with me on the project, most of whom provided support and good humor throughout.

> I can't say when I'll use these skills again, but I do know that there's little chance that the situation will be as rewarding or as fun as the one in which I learned them.

We spent three weeks in the Idaho Panhandle National Forest, building bridges, carving new trails through the forest, and clearing away fallen trees and brush from the old trails. "We" were an Australian woman, five German men, a French man and woman, a British woman, and two American women besides myself. The whole experience was rewarding in so many ways that I shrink at attempting to categorize them, but I will say I learned a lot—not the least of which was how to use a Pulaski. For the uninitiated, a Pulaski is a combination axe/hoe, the sharpness of which is in inverse proportion to the pain it creates in the wielder's back. The sharpener broke the week before we arrived.

Nicole Ellison (far left) with international volunteers on a CIEE workcamp in Bonner's Ferry, Idaho.

The town in which we worked was a small (pop. 2,200) working-class town a half an hour by car from Canada and home to some of the most stunning forested areas I have ever seen. Almost all of the population of Bonner's Ferry is supported, directly or indirectly, by the timber industry. Before the camp, my feelings about the timber debate were largely theoretical. I soon realized that, like all political questions, it was not so simple. Many of the people in Bonner's Ferry depended upon the timber industry for their survival, as was evident by the number of signs reading, "This household supported by the timber industry." The local bar went one step further—above the counter hung a bumper sticker that read, "Spotted owl tastes like chicken." One of the rangers that worked with us was a logger in the wintertime. The yearly switch from preserving trees to cutting them down clearly pained his conscience, but logging was the only way he could support his family and still live in the area he loved.

Although there were trying moments—mostly stemming from the few members of the group who made little effort to interact with the rest of us—all in all we had a lot of fun. The work was physically difficult; but it's amazing how little it takes to get someone to laugh hysterically when you're both exhausted from menial labor. But we laughed a lot even when we weren't working, aided by the comedians in our group. Knut, a German pre-med student, soon became infamous for his skeleton jokes, some of which made the transition to English better than others. (Example: a skeleton went to a doctor to ask for advice. "You're too late," said the doctor.) We'd get back from work around 4:30 and sit outside our house or by the dock drinking beers 'till dinner, chewing the fat, writing postcards, and bragging about the bridge we'd built that day. We drank huckleberry shakes and taught Knut English colloquialisms. "It bites the big one, ja?" he'd ask, usually at appropriate moments. And we did have our disasters. One woman was thrown from a horse and broke her arm; someone's sock clogged the water pump; the liquor store was closed all day Sunday.

During the first and third weeks we would show up at the ranger station at 7:30 a.m. and ride, in various transport rigs, to worksites an hour or so away. The second week we camped, hiking to a secluded area 13 miles out. The ranger in charge insisted on "low impact" camping, which basically means leaving as little evidence of your stay as possible—though we didn't, as my step-father thought, have to eat our coffee grounds; nor is it, as my mother wondered, related to low-impact aerobics.

Building bridges was especially rewarding because it involved putting to use principles that up 'till then had been mere abstractions. The idea of a gradient, for example, becomes more than a mathematical concept when you are trying to walk up it. I now know the difference between horse trails and people trails, how far a sill has to be buried in the ground to be stable, what kind of trees will survive transplanting, and the best way to wrench a boulder the size of a large TV set out of the ground (hint: you need more than one person). I can't say when I'll use these skills again, but I do know that there's little chance that the situation will be as rewarding or as fun as the one in which I learned them.

PART THREE
Short-Term Projects

All-Union Student Brigade

Bolkonsomoliski Per 7/8
101000 Moscow
Russia

Organization: The All-Union Student Brigade promotes workcamp exchanges between youth from the U.S. and Russia.
Program: Volunteers work in either rural or urban environments, performing such tasks as fruit harvesting and church reconstruction.
Requirements: None.
Age: Minimum 18.
Living Arrangements: Volunteers live in tent camps in rural locations and in student hostels in cities.
Finances: Volunteers pay a placement fee to the national workcamp organization in their own country. The All-Union Student Brigade charges a fee of approximately $400, which covers lodging, meals, and all transportation costs upon arrival in Moscow.
Deadline: April 15.
Contact: U.S. volunteers must apply through the Council on International Educational Exchange (see the organization's listing in this section).

American Farm School/ Summer Work Activities Program

1133 Broadway at 26th Street
New York, NY 10010
Phone: (212) 463-8434

Organization: The Farm School is an agricultural high school for youth from farming families all over Greece.
Program: Volunteers work on the farm in Thessaloniki, Greece, for eight weeks during the summer; they bale and store hay, harvest the wheat crop, work in the nursery and greenhouse, help maintain the tractors, milk cows, and do landscaping.
Requirements: Agriculture students having practical experience with both crops and livestock are preferred.
Age: College graduates and undergraduates from any country.
Living Arrangements: Participants live in dormitories; they receive approximately $15 per day and must pay for their own meals.
Persons with Disabilities: "Due to the nature of the program, participation by persons with disabilities would unfortunately not be possible."
Finances: Room is provided.
Deadline: March 1.
Contact: Maria Lozada, Program Coordinator.

American Friends Service Committee

1501 Cherry Street
Philadelphia, PA 19102
Phone: (215) 241-7000

Organization: AFSC is a Quaker organization which "undertakes programs of relief, service and education, ministering to both spiritual and physical needs. We reject war, violence and exploitation as unjustifiable violations of human rights and dignity."
Program: AFSC has sponsored short-term community service projects in

Latin America since 1939. Each year approximately 50 volunteers live in and work with a rural community; most projects run from the end of June to mid-August. Work includes the construction and repair of schools, clinics, roads, houses and irrigation systems. Projects involve 10 volunteers and two leaders. Generally, half the group is Latin American. In addition, there is a project in Cuba in cooperation with a Baptist group during July. This project combines group work (usually in sugar cane fields) with study, discussion groups, recreation, and cultural events.
Requirements: Construction, gardening, arts, crafts, or childcare experience is helpful. Spanish is absolutely essential since it is spoken at all times during the project.
Age: 18–26.
Living Arrangements: The group lives together and shares housework, often in a school or other village building.
Finances: For the Mexican-Latin American project, participants contribute $700 which covers orientation, room and board, and health and accident insurance. Limited scholarship aid is available. The cost of the Cuban program is the sum of round-trip transportation, visas and incidental expenses, and a $250 fee.
Deadline: March 15.
Contact: Hilda Grauman, Personnel Services Coordinator, Latin America Summer Project.

"The work (in Cuba) was hot and fairly strenuous for those not accustomed to field work, but the hours flew by happily with plenty of singing, jesting and conversations ranging in topics from music to Marx, as we explored the differences and similarities in the ways we live."

American Hiking Society

P.O. Box 20160
Washington, DC 20041
Phone: (703) 385-3252

Organization: AHS is dedicated to protecting the interests of hikers and preserving America's footpaths.
Program: AHS sponsors Volunteer Vacation Programs. Each year, 25 to 30 two-week trips are scheduled. A few are held during the winter months in Florida, Hawaii, and the Virgin Islands. Participants build trails and do maintenance work in national parks and forests where there are no local trail clubs to do the work. Teams of 10 to 12 people work for 10 days; if the project is in a remote area, the team works out of a base camp for the entire period; at more accessible projects, the team may camp and work during the week but will hike out for the weekend.
Requirements: Volunteers must be experienced hikers (able to walk 5 to 10 miles per day with ease). Volunteers should be able to do hard manual work at high altitudes.
Age: Minimum 16; 13 with an adult.
Living Arrangements: Volunteers provide their own gear—tents, backpacks, etc.
Finances: There's a $30 fee for participation. Volunteers must provide their own transportation to and from the site. In most cases, food is provided by the hosts or a donor.
Deadline: None.

Contact: AHS, Volunteer Vacations, P.O. Box 86, North Scituate, MA 02060. Include a self-addressed, stamped envelope for information.

American Jewish Society for Service

15 East 26th Street
New York, NY 10010
Phone: (212) 683-6178

Organization: AJSS was founded in 1950 "to give Jews and those of other faiths an opportunity to perform humanitarian service in fulfillment of the highest teachings of Judaism." To do this, AJSS sponsors two or three workcamps each summer for high school juniors and seniors.
Program: AJSS workcamps take place all over the U.S.; they last for seven weeks and begin July 1. In 1991, three camps were held: one in Chicago, Illinois; one in Topeka, Kansas; and one in Everett, Washington. The campers repaired and improved homes of low income homeowners. In the past, projects have included constructing facilities at camps for underprivileged children, building homes in a self-help housing project, repairing flood and tornado damage, etc. Each workcamp has a director, two counselors, a cook, and a group of about 16 volunteers. In addition to the work the volunteers do, there's a social, recreational, and educational component to the program—there are meetings with local teachers, discussions of Judaism, and trips to points of interest near the project. The workcamp session is preceded by a June orientation meeting for volunteers and their parents.
Requirements: No special skills are required—"only the willingness to live simply and cooperatively and to do work that is sometimes strenuous and commonplace."
Age: 16–18.
Living Arrangements: Volunteers usually live in a school or large house.
Persons with Disabilities: Volunteers with disabilities who are capable of doing construction work would be considered.
Finances: There's a $1,000 fee which covers room and board. (This is less than half of the actual cost which is provided by individual foundation contributions.) Spending money and transportation are the responsibility of the volunteer. Some scholarships are available.
Deadline: June 1.
Contact: Henry Kohn, Chairman.

"I feel that what I have done has not only changed the lives of the ones we helped, but it has changed my whole outlook on what we are doing and why we are here."

Amigos de las Americas

5618 Star Lane
Houston, TX 77057
Phone: (800) 231-7796

Organization: Amigos is an international development organization that works in public health projects throughout Latin America. All of its work is done in collaboration with the host country's ministry of health. Since its founding in 1965, more than 15,500 volunteers have served. The

head office of Amigos is in Houston; from there the projects themselves and the chapters of 20 local training groups are coordinated.
Program: Young people spend four to eight weeks as summer volunteers in villages in Brazil, Costa Rica, the Dominican Republic, Ecuador, Mexico, and Paraguay. The goals of the volunteers are improved health and longer lives for the people with whom they work. Projects involve animal health, community sanitation, immunization, vision health, dental hygiene, well digging, community development, and other service areas. Every volunteer must complete four to six months of training organized by their local chapters. The training program includes conversational Spanish, Latin American culture and history, public health care skills, human relations, and problem solving. In 1991, 560 young people participated in the program.
Requirements: Amigos is "for dynamic young adults who are excited about helping others... You need a sense of adventure and enthusiasm, a willingness to take responsibility and work hard and a healthy dose of self-discipline."
Age: Minimum 16.
Living Arrangements: Volunteers live with local families or are housed in schools or clinics; the mayor, local doctor, or town priest see to the volunteers' daily needs.
Finances: Volunteers pay $2,200-$2,900, depending on their assignment, most of which is raised through local fund raising efforts.
Deadline: March 1.
Contact: Director of Recruiting.

"I've learned about another culture, its people and language...but, more than anything else, I've learned about me."

Andover Foundation for Archaeological Research

P.O. Box 83
Andover, MA 01810
Phone: (508) 470-0840

Organization: AFAR performs archaeological research in the American Southwest and Central America.
Program: Students and Friends of the Foundation accompany professional archaeologists on expeditions, learning and using the latest techniques in field and lab work. Programs last two to four weeks, or 14 weeks.
Requirements: Participants on the 14-week program must have completed some college-level archaeological coursework.
Age: Minimum 16.
Living Arangements: Volunteers live in simple housing.
Finances: Friends of the Foundation make a $1500 tax-exempt contribution for the short programs. The 14-week program requires a contribution of $3000. Room and board is provided.
Deadline: December 1.
Contact: R.S. MacNeish.

Annunciation House

1003 East San Antonio
El Paso, TX 79901
Phone: (915) 545-4509

Organization: Annunciation House is a private organization founded 14

years ago, with the belief that "the Gospel calls us all to the poor." It operates several houses on either side of the U.S.-Mexico border, in the cities of El Paso and Juarez, offering hospitality to the homeless, particularly Central American refugees and the undocumented. Annunciation House comes out of a Catholic tradition and operates from a Christian faith perspective.
Program: Volunteers are needed to staff emergency and homeless shelters, to provide immigration/refugee services to Hispanics, to construct and maintain buildings, and to provide health care and social services. Annunciation House sponsors a 10-week Summer Internship Program in addition to the year-long positions it offers.
Requirements: A college degree and knowledge of Spanish are very helpful but not mandatory. It is important for volunteers to realize that they must be open to doing whatever needs to be done.
Age: Minimum 19.
Living Arrangements: Volunteers live in dormitory-style rooms set aside for staff.
Persons with Disabilities: Each applicant is considered individually.
Finances: Room, board, minor medical expenses, washing machines, and personal items are provided.
Deadline: Two weeks prior to one of the specific arrival dates for new volunteers: January 20, March 20, June 1, August 15, and November 1.
Contact: Ruben L. Garcia, Director, or Sr. Stella Dolan, Volunteer Coordinator.

"Annunciation House is a place to reconnect with what's important in life. I have learned more here in this one month than I have learned in the rest of my life."

Appalachian Trail Conference

P.O. Box 807
Harper's Ferry, WV 25425-0807
Phone: (304) 535-6331

Organization: The purpose of the Appalachian Trail Conference is to maintain and protect the Appalachian Trail, which extends for 2,100 miles from Maine to Georgia.
Program: Volunteers are needed during the summer and fall to perform such tasks as trail construction and rehabilitation, shelter and bridge construction, and open areas management. Participants work in crews of six to eight, supervised by a trained leader. Opportunities can last from one week to the entire season (June through October).
Requirements: Volunteers must be in good physical condition.
Age: Minimum 18.
Living Arrangements: Volunteers share living quarters in the field, primarily in tent camps. Two days each week are spent at the base camp.
Persons with Disabilities: Must be able to perform physical labor.
Finances: Volunteers receive room, board, and insurance.
Deadline: Applications are available in February and are accepted until each crew is filled.
Contact: Crews.

Architects and Planners in Support of Nicaragua

P.O. Box 1151
Topanga, CA 90290-1151
Phone: (213) 455-1340

Organization: For seven years, APSNICA has sponsored volunteers of all skill levels in building and economic development in Nicaragua.
Program: Professionals are needed to provide technical assistance in a number of fields. Volunteers are also needed to form work brigades.
Requirements: None.
Age: The average age of participants is 25.
Living Arrangements: Volunteers live with Nicaraguan families.
Persons with Disabilites: Persons with disabilities are welcome as long as they can cope with the physical hardship of life in Nicaragua.
Finances: There is a program fee of $300. Travel, room and board, and all other personal costs are the volunteer's responsibility.
Deadline: None.

Association Culturelle des Activités d'Amitié et d'Echange entre Jeunes

Cité de l'Enfance
Palais du Peuples
Place de Premier Mai
Algers, Algeria

Organization: ACAAEJ organizes workcamps in Algeria to promote social and cultural interaction among young people.
Program: Volunteers work in projects that include environment protection, development of playgrounds and open spaces, restoration of rural schools, and the construction of socio-educational centers and children's camps. Activities include maintenance, construction, painting, masonry, and reforestation.
Requirements: No special skills are required, but skilled volunteers in the areas mentioned previously are encouraged to apply.
Age: Minimum 18.
Living Arrangements: Lodging is provided on the workcamp site. Living conditions are simple. Volunteers should bring sleeping bags.
Persons with Disabilities: Disabled persons should write in advance to find out if a particular camp features accessible worksites.
Finances: Volunteers pay a placement fee to the national workcamp organization in their own country. Room and board are provided, but the cost of travel to and from the workcamp is the volunteer's responsibility.
Deadline: April 15.
Contact: Volunteers must apply through a national workcamp organization in their own country. For further information, U.S. volunteers should contact the Council on International Educational Exchange (see the organization's listing in this section).

Association of Volunteers for Service in Protected Areas

Apartado 10104-1000
San José, Costa Rica
Phone: (506) 23-69-63

Organization: ASVO is a nonprofit, nongovernmental organization dedicated to training volunteers for service in the 26 areas set aside by Costa Rica for the conservation of natural resources.
Program: ASVO offers an Occasional Volunteer Program for foreigners and Costa Rican citizens interested in working with the National Park Service for periods of two months and up. Duties include construction, maintenance, investigatory work, and environmental education (though educational and investigative programs are geared toward volunteers intending to work for a more extended period).
Requirements: No previous experience or degrees are necessary for construction and maintenance; environmental education and investigatory work do require training appropriate to the project. All volunteers should have a good command of Spanish.
Age: Minimum 16.
Living Arrangements: Volunteers live in the homes of park workers. Conditions are basic.
Finances: Volunteers pay a fee of $300 a month, which covers room and board, local transportation, and administrative costs.
Deadline: None.
Contact: Stanley Arguedas, Director, Programa Voluntariado.

Association Tunisienne d'Action Volontaire

Maison du R.C.D.
Boulevard 9 Avril 1938
Tunis, Tunisia

Organization: ATAV organizes workcamps in Tunisia.
Program: Volunteers work in projects that include construction, nature conservation, and development of youth cultural centers and schools.
Requirements: No special skills are required.
Age: Minimum 18.
Living Arrangements: Lodging is provided on the workcamp site. Living conditions are simple.
Persons with Disabilities: Disabled persons should write in advance to find out if a particular camp features accessible worksites.
Finances: Volunteers pay a placement fee to the national workcamp organization in their country. Room and board are provided, but the cost of travel to and from the workcamp is the volunteer's responsibility.
Deadline: April 15.
Contact: Volunteers must apply through a national workcamp organization in their own country. For further information, U.S. volunteers should contact the Council on International Educational Exchange (see the organization's listing in this section).

Australian Trust for Conservation Volunteers

P.O. Box 423
Ballarat
Victoria, Australia 3350
Phone: (61-53) 327-490

Organization: ATCV is a community-based, nonprofit, nonpolitical organization promoting voluntary participation in tasks that benefit the natural environment.
Program: Volunteers spend six weeks (or more under special circumstances), planting trees, doing erosion control work, and fence construction. Assignments may be in New South Wales, Victoria, and South Australia, and are available year round. ATCV's latest program, the ACTV Echidna Package, is a working holiday enabling volunteers to experience Australia inexpensively while at the same time being involved in practical conservation tasks.
Requirements: No special skills are required.
Age: Minimum 17.
Finances: The fee for the program is AU$450 for six weeks and then AU$50 per week for the next six weeks. This covers the costs of food, accommodation, and travel while on the task.
Living Arrangements: Depending on the location and nature of the task, you might stay in farm houses, shearers' quarters, trailers, or tents.
Deadline: None.

Bangladesh Work Camps Association

289/2 Work Camp Road, North Shajahanpur, GPO Box 3974
Dhaka 1217, Bangladesh
Phone: (880-2) 40-34-79

Organization: BWCA is a voluntary youth organization with no political or government affiliation which has been in existence since 1958.
Program: BWCA organizes workcamps all over the country from October to April. The projects involve building houses, constructing roads, providing health care to rural youths, etc. Up to now, few U.S. participants have worked in BWCA projects, but they are definitely welcome.
Requirements: No special skills are required.
Age: 15–45.
Living Arrangements: Volunteers stay at a campsite along with local people.
Finances: Room and board and domestic travel costs are provided.
Deadline: September.
Contact: Abdur Rahman, Organizing Secretary.

Boys Hope

4200 Ripa
St. Louis, MO 63125
Phone: (314) 544-1250

Organization: Boys Hope was founded in 1977 in Saint Louis, Missouri, to serve abused, abandoned, and neglected youth. The mission of Boys Hope is to provide a family-like home environment and Jesuit-influenced college preparatory education to capable and needy youths. The program is presently operative in 11 locations: Chicago; Cincinnati; Cleveland; Detroit; New Orleans; New York; Northeast Ohio; Orange County, California; Phoenix; Pittsburgh; and St. Louis. Boys join the program when they are between 10 and 14 and can remain with Boys Hope through high school.

Program: In addition to year-long volunteer opportunities in its homes, Boys Hope operates Camp Owakonze during the summers on Baril Lake in Ontario, Canada. Volunteers are needed as camp counselors from mid-June to early August.

Requirements: Volunteers must have some experience with camping or sports.

Age: Minimum 18.

Living Arrangements: Volunteers are provided with cabin-style quarters.

Finances: Room and board and a small stipend are provided.

Deadline: April 15.

Contact: Fr. Paul Sheridan

Canadian Bureau for International Education

85 Albert Street, Suite 1400
Ottawa, Ontario K1P 6A4
Canada

Organization: CBIE promotes international development and intercultural understanding through a variety of programs, one of which is the international workcamp it organizes annually.

Program: CBIE's workcamps in Canada consist of a group of 8 to 20 young people who work together on a community project for three to four weeks during July and/or August. A typical example is the workcamp hosted by the Nipissing Indian Band of the Ojibuay. Volunteers worked on the restoration of St. Leonard's Church, a 100-year old landmark on the Nipissing Indian Reserve. Tasks included painting, scraping, applying wood preservation, etc. Participants live in native homes.

Requirements: No special skills are necessary.

Age: Minimum 18.

Finances: Volunteers pay a placement fee to the national workcamp organization in their own country. Room and board are provided, but the cost of travel to and from the workcamp is the volunteer's responsibility.

Deadline: April 15.

Contact: Volunteers must apply through a national workcamp organization in their own country. For further information, U.S. volunteers must contact either the Council on International Educational Exchange or Volunteers for Peace (see these organizations' listings in this section).

Caribbean Conservation Corporation

P.O. Box 2866
Gainesville, FL 32602-2866
Phone: (904) 373-6441

Organization: CCC is a nonprofit organization engaged in research, conservation, and education toward the

preservation of the natural environment of such endangered species as the sea turtle.
Program: The "Turtles of Tortuguero" program encompasses a variety of volunteer field research activities. Programs last for 10 or 17 days during the spring and summer. Volunteers may choose between studying Leatherback and Freshwater Turtles or tagging Green Sea Turtles.
Requirements: None.
Living Arrangements: Volunteers live in a rustic bunkhouse at the project field station
Persons with Disabilities: All are welcome as long as they can walk several miles a night along the nesting beaches.
Finances: Program fees are in the $1,500 to $2,000 range. This covers round-trip airfare between Miami and San José, all scheduled transportation in Costa Rica, and room and board.
Deadline: Reservations are accepted on a first-come, first-served basis.
Contact: Massachusetts Audubon Society, Natural History Travel, Lincoln, MA 01773; (800) 289-9504.

Carrefour Canadien International

2520 LeClaire
Montreal, Québec
Canada
Phone (514) 251-0685

Organization: This nonprofit cultural exchange organization arranges multinational volunteer work programs in Canada.

Program: Volunteers work for eight weeks during the summer. Projects areas include agriculture, community service, development, education, and health care.
Requirements: Participants must speak French.
Age: Minimum 19.
Living Arrangements: In local facilities or with families.
Finances: A fee of approximately CAN$1,500 covers room, board, and insurance.
Deadline: October 15.

Catholic Medical Mission Board

10 West 17th Street
New York, NY 10011-5765
Phone: (212) 242-7757

Organization: CMMB ships medicine to 6,000 missions in 60 Third World countries and recruits and processes volunteer medical personnel for service, without remuneration, to Third World missions for periods of one month to two or more years.
Program: Medical personnel are stationed in Africa, Asia, the Caribbean, Central and South America, India, and Oceania.
Requirements: A degree in medicine, dentistry, or technology. State licenses are required for nurses. Language requirements depend upon location.
Living Arrangements: Depending on the individual mission, accommodations are provided either on the mission compound or nearby.
Persons with Disabilities: CMMB accepts persons with disabilities if the

disability permits service at the mission.
Finances: Volunteers receive room and board. Those who serve six months or more usually receive a modest stipend. Insurance is the responsibility of missions capable of providing such services.
Deadline: None.
Contact: Leo T. Tarpey, Placement Director.

Centre for Youth and Social Development

A-70 Saheed Nagar
Bhubaneswar-751 007
Orissa, India

Organization: CYSD is a national organization engaged in multisectoral development activities such as research, training, and dissemination of development resource information.
Program: Volunteers are needed to work in the Indian state of Orissa for one week to six months. Possible opportunities include conducting youth leadership camps, providing health care and family planning services, planning and implementation of village development programs, and teaching.
Requirements: Volunteers should be physically strong and have working experience in the above fields. Knowledge of English is required. Hindi and Oriya are helpful.
Age: Volunteers "should be young."
Living Arrangements: Modest board and lodging facilities are available.
Finances: Volunteers provide for their own expenses.
Deadline: None.
Contact: Mr. Jagadananda, Member-Secretary.

Chantiers Jeunesse Maroc

B P. 1351
R P. Rabat, Morocco

Organization: CJM organizes workcamps in Morocco and also places volunteers abroad. Its goals include promoting contact and exchange among youth of different countries.
Program: Volunteers work on projects that will contribute to the development of disadvantaged communities. Activities may include building restoration, construction, and painting.
Requirements: No special skills are required.
Age: Minimum 18.
Living Arrangements: Lodging is provided. Living conditions are simple.
Persons with Disabilities: Disabled persons should write in advance to inquire about accessible worksites.
Finances: Volunteers pay a placement fee to the national workcamp organization in their country. Room and board are provided, but the cost of travel to and from the workcamp is the volunteer's responsibility.
Deadline: April 15.
Contact: Volunteers must apply through a national workcamp organization in their own country. For further information, U.S. volunteers should contact the Council on International Educational Exchange or Volunteers for Peace (see these organizations' listings in this section).

Christian Welfare and Social Relief

39 Soldier Street
Box 981
Freetown, Sierra Leone

Organization: CWASR is a nonprofit rural youth workcamp organization established in 1980.
Program: Workcamps are offered throughout rural Sierra Leone. Volunteers may serve from three weeks to three months, providing such services as adult education, construction, and social work.
Requirements: None.
Age: 11–45.
Living Arrangements: Volunteers live in camps, hostels, or private homes.
Finances: Volunteers pay a registration fee of $600. Room and board are provided.
Deadline: None.
Contact: Miss Ayo Thomas, Camp Coordinator.

CKM/KMC

Malostranske nabrezi 1
11000 Prague 1
Czechoslovakia

Organization: CKM is the youth travel bureau of Czechoslovakia; one of its activities is the organization of workcamps.
Program: CKM workcamps take place for two or three weeks in July, August, and September in big cities and in the country. Last year, volunteers were involved in construction, archaeology, agriculture, and conservation; they made a path through the mountains, worked in a zoo, reconstructed a junior camp, built a social center, helped with a harvest at a farm hostel, repaired a mountain chalet, worked to maintain equipment at a winter sports center, and helped reconstruct a castle, among other things. In order to insure a true mix of people, only three volunteers from any one country can work on a project. English is the most widely spoken language at the camps. Evening and weekend activities are arranged for participants, including lectures, excursions to local industrial and agricultural plants, and meetings with local young people and families.
Requirements: None.
Age: 18–35.
Living Arrangements: Volunteers may live in youth hostels or student dormitories.
Persons with Disabilities: Generally, persons with disabilities are not accepted, however, it usually depends on the individual abilities of such volunteers.
Finances: Volunteers pay a placement fee to the national workcamp organization in their own country. Room and board are provided, but the cost of travel to and from the workcamp is the volunteer's responsibility.
Deadline: April 15.
Contact: Volunteers must apply through a national workcamp organization in their own country. For further information, U.S. volunteers must contact either the Council on International Educational Exchange or Volunteers for Peace (see these organizations' listings in this section).

Club du Vieux Manoir

10, rue de la Cossonnerie
75001 Paris, France
Phone: (33-14) 45.08.80.40

Organization: Club du Vieux Manoir is involved with the rescue and restoration of historical sites—gardens, fortresses, and churches throughout France.
Program: Most workcamps take place during Easter vacation and the summer, but three operate year round. During the summer, volunteers stay at least five days, beginning on the 2nd or 16th day of the month.
Age: Minimum 14.
Living Arrangements: Camping facilities are provided.
Finances: Volunteers pay a daily room and board fee and a small application fee.

Colorado Trail Foundation

548 Pine Song Trail
Golden, CO 80401
Phone: (303) 526-0809

Organization: The Colorado Trail Foundation has been working on building the Colorado Trail—a 480-mile trail that reaches from Denver to Durango. This group also builds and maintains other trails in the national forests of Colorado.
Program: Volunteers work for one week or more in June, July, or August. Crews begin work on Saturdays, and depending upon the remoteness of the work location, go by jeep, car, or bike to the base camp. Sunday mornings are spent in safety instruction

Club du Vieux Manoir volunteers excavating wall foundations at Chateau Philippe le Bel, in France.

and an introduction to trailbuilding skills. Crews work an eight-hour day Monday, Tuesday, Thursday, and Friday. Wednesday and Sunday afternoons are free for biking, fishing, and enjoying the wilderness. If you sign up for two or more consecutive weeks, the Saturday and Sunday between weeks are also free for enjoying the surroundings.
Requirements: Anyone in good physical condition is welcome.
Age: The minimum is 16 unless you are accompanied by a parent.
Living Arrangements: Volunteers sleep in tents and must provide their own sleeping bags, tents and eating utensils; cooking utensils, food, hard hats, tools and supplies are furnished by Friends of the Colorado Trail and the Forest Service.
Finances: There is a registration fee of

$25 per person; board is provided.
Deadline: May 15.
Contact: Trail Crew Coordinator.

Compagnons Bâtisseurs

rue Notre-Dame de Graces, 63
6900 Marche-en-Famenne
Belgium

Organization: Compagnons organizes international workcamps in Belgium.
Program: All projects in Belgium are construction and building renovation projects.
Requirements: Although English and French are both accepted languages for the Belgian workcamps, U.S. participants are strongly advised to have some knowledge of French to allow optimal interaction.
Age: Minimum 18.
Living Arrangements: Volunteers spend a night in Brussels and then live at the workcamp site.
Finances: Volunteers pay a placement fee to the national workcamp organization in their own country. Room and board are provided, but the cost of travel to and from the workcamp is the volunteer's responsibility.
Deadline: April 15.
Contact: Volunteers must apply through a national workcamp organization in their own country. For further information, U.S. volunteers should contact the Council on International Educational Exchange (see the organization's listing in this section).

Concordia

38 rue du Fauborg St. Denis
75010 Paris
France

Organization: Concordia is a French organization which has been involved in voluntary service and international exchange for 40 years.
Program: Concordia's workcamps take place for two to three weeks during spring, summer, and fall. The organization operates adult workcamps for people 18 and over and teenage camps for youths over 15. Projects take place all over France and involve construction, restoration, conservation, or social work. Each workcamp includes 5 French volunteers and 10 from other countries.
Requirements: No special skills for the short-term camps; long-term assignments require some construction skills.
Living Arrangements: Volunteers usually live in a school or similar public building in conditions that are "rustic but adequate."
Persons with Disabilities: Volunteers with minor disabilities are accepted.
Finances: Volunteers pay a placement fee to the national workcamp organization in their own country. Room and board are provided, but the cost of travel to and from the workcamp is the volunteer's responsibility.
Deadline: April 15.
Contact: Volunteers must apply through a national workcamp organization in their own country. For further information, U.S. volunteers

must contact the Council on International Educational Exchange (see the organization's listing in this section).

"I had a great time and learned a lot of skills, language, etc...the first few days were really hard getting along with the people, but by the end, I had many friends from the area and fellow volunteers."

Council on International Educational Exchange

International Voluntary Service Department
205 East 42nd Street
New York, NY 10017
Phone: (212) 661-1414, ext. 1139

Organization: CIEE is a membership organization of over 200 colleges, universities, secondary schools, and youth-serving agencies. It is the co-publisher of *Volunteer!*

Program: One of CIEE's many activities is the organization of workcamps in the U.S. and the placement of American volunteers in workcamps in Africa, Europe, and North America. Since 1984, CIEE has offered three-week projects for groups of 10 to 15 volunteers—American and foreign—in July and August. Volunteers have assisted in park maintenance and conservation efforts in Yosemite and Golden Gate National Parks. Other projects have included an archaeological dig in western Kentucky and neighborhood revitalization projects in New York. Through cooperation with partner organizations, CIEE places Americans in projects in Algeria, Belgium, Bulgaria, Canada, Czechoslovakia, Denmark, France, Germany, Ghana, Hungary, Ireland, Morocco, the Netherlands, Poland, Portugal, Spain, Tunisia, Turkey, Wales, and republics of the former Soviet Union, and is currently developing exchanges with more African countries.

Requirements: None.
Age: Minimum 18.
Living Arrangements: Volunteers live together in student hostels or tents.
Finances: A fee of $125 covers administrative costs. Room and board are provided.
Deadline: April 15.

CIEE workcamp participants in La Roche sur Grane, France, where they renovated the path to a 15th-century hamlet.

"I made lifetime friends who helped me to see the world in a different way. This was truly a fantastic experience with people and events that I'll never forget."

Crow Canyon Archaeological Center

23390 County Road K
Cortez, CO 81321
Phone: (800) 422-8975

Organization: Located in southwestern Colorado, Crow Canyon is a nonprofit organization dedicated to archaeological research and education, where lay people participate with archaeologists in scientific research.
Program: Crow Canyon offers a number of different programs during its five-month season from June through October. Participants assist with archaeological fieldwork, laboratory analysis, and environmental fieldwork. Programs last a minimum of one week, with the option to stay on up to the end of the season. Crow Canyon's High School Field School lasts four weeks.
Requirements: None.
Age: Participants must be 14 by March 1 of the program year.
Living Arrangements: Shared accommodations in dorm facilities or in small cabins. Shared bath facilities are modern.
Persons with Disabilities: Persons with disabilities are welcomed, but field experiences may be limited depending upon the disability.
Finances: Fees range from $500 to $750 a week. The price includes room and board and all other program expenses.
Deadline: Applications are accepted until programs are filled.
Contact: Lynn Dyer, Director of Marketing.

Dorset Natural History and Archaeological Society

Dorset County Museum
High West Street
Dorchester, Dorset DT1 1XA
England

Organization: The Society is a charitable trust which is concerned with geology, natural history, archaeology, local history, biography, literature, and the arts of Dorset.
Program: Volunteers participate in archaeological excavations for a week to a month at a time, usually from April to September.
Requirements: Participants must have "patience, discipline, and an ability to learn."
Persons with Disabilities: There are limited possibilities.
Finances: Volunteers pay all their own expenses.
Deadline: None.
Contact: R.N. Peters, Curator.

Earthstewards Network

P.O. Box 10697
Bainbridge Island, WA 98110
Phone: (206) 842-7986/9353

Organization: The Earthstewards Network is an environmental youth service organizaton that coordinates international environmental workcamps in western North America and Central America. This environmental workcamp program, called Peace Trees, began with a 1988 effort which brought U.S. and Soviet youth together in southern India.

Program: Peace Trees operates in watershed coastal and urban areas throughout the Cascadian range in the U.S. Northwest and British Columbia. It also operates in Costa Rica with possible upcoming projects in Mexico, Nicaragua, and Panama. Projects include soil conservation, rural and urban reforestation, trail construction, stream rehabilitation, urban greenways and parks.
Requirements: None.
Age: 17–23. Some coordinator positions are available for older volunteers.
Living Arrangements: Group camps and/or homestays.
Persons with Disabilities: There are opportunities for individuals with a wide range of personal interests and abilities.
Finances: Overseas volunteers will be expected to fundraise between $500 and $1,500. This will cover room and board, travel, and administrative fees, and will help to sponsor low-income international participants. Some scholarships are available. Fees for North American projects vary according to the programs and available resources of local partner organizations. Insurance is provided for all overseas projects and some North American projects.
Deadline: None. Projects are run in the summer; early application simplifies planning and allows more time for fundraising.
Contact: Dwight Wilson or Angus Murdoch, Project Coordinators.

Earthwatch

680 Mount Auburn Street
P.O. Box 403N
Watertown, MA 02272
Phone: (617) 926-8200

Organization: Earthwatch, founded in 1971, recruits volunteers to join research scientists in archaeology, marine biology, animal behavior, ecology, and anthropology projects all over the world.
Program: Expeditions take place year round. In Indonesia an Earthwatch group researches traditional healthcare practices; in New Zealand they explore and measure the inner workings of a volcano; in Costa Rica they survey the behavior of dolphins.
Requirements: Participants must be Earthwatch members; annual membership fee is $25
Age: Minimum 16.
Living Arrangements: Range from university dorms to tents, research stations, or old castles.
Finances: Projects cost from $800 to $2,000. This tax-deductible donation to the expedition covers room and board, ground transportation, and equipment.
Deadline: None.

Eclaireuses et Eclaireurs du Senegal

5, rue Pierre Millon
P.O. Box 744
Dakar, Senegal
Phone: (221) 27 73 67

Organization: This Senegalese youth organization is affiliated with the

World Organization of Scout Movements.
Program: EES offers summer workcamps lasting one to three months; other positions, however, are available throughout the year. Work may include construction, training, agriculture, health, and environmental protection.
Requirements: No special skills are required, but EES looks for people with backgrounds in administration, agriculture, child care, teaching, training, and public relations. French is useful but not compulsory.
Age: Minimum 18.
Persons with Disabilities: Persons with disabilities are accepted and usually offered administrative tasks.
Finances: EES provides lodging, but volunteers are responsible for all other costs.
Deadline: Volunteers must apply by December for each following year.
Contact: Lamine Diawara, National Commissioner for Administration.

Ecumenical Young Adult Ministry Staff Team

475 Riverside Drive
New York, NY 10115
Phone: (212) 870-2297

Organization: EYAMST is a coalition of young adult ministry staff persons of national denominations brought together for cooperative and ecumenical projects.
Program: EYAMST co-sponsors (with the International Christian Youth Exchange) workcamps/study tours in the Southern Hemisphere as part of its commitment to global justice. Volunteers spend a month of both physical work and in-depth cultural awareness. Emphasis is placed on reciprocal learning and on an analysis of the socio-economic milieu in which the workcamp project exists.
Requirements: None.
Age: 18–30.
Living Arrangements: Group housing in the workcamp site village.
Persons with Disabilities: Open to persons with disabilities.
Finances: The cost of the workcamps and study tours ranges from $2,510 to $2,700. This fee includes pre-departure and in-country orientations, transportation, cultural and social presentations and interactions, room and board, medical insurance, evaluation, and in-country transportation. EYAMST members provide scholarships for persons from member denominations. ICYE also provides scholarship assistance (see ICYE's listing in this section).
Deadline: First applicant screening held February 15, with subsequent screenings held on March 15 and April 15—based on available placements.
Contact: International Christian Youth Exchange (see this organization's listing in this section).

Esperança

1911 West Earll Drive
Phoenix, AZ 85015
Phone: (602) 252-7772

Organization: Esperança is a nonprofit, nondenominational international health agency which includes

clinical services in the Amazon of Brazil.
Program: Esperança sends volunteer surgical teams with expertise in the fields of plastic surgery, orthopedics, and ophthalmology. These teams serve for two to three weeks and are sent six times a year.
Requirements: Volunteers must be board-certified surgeons, anesthesiologists, or surgical nurses. Fluency in Spanish or Portuguese is preferred.
Living Arrangements: Comfortable, semi-private quarters with running water, electricity, and good food.
Persons with Disabilities: There is no specific policy. Individuals must be able to function within the confines of the Amazon location.
Finances: Room and board are provided.
Deadline: None.
Contact: William V. Dolan.

Ethnic and Cultural Practicum

Indiana University
321 Education Building
Bloomington, IN 47405
Phone: (812) 855-8579

Organization: Each summer the University of Indiana conducts a course on Navajo, Apache, and Hopi reservations in the Southwest. Study and voluntary service is combined and graduate and undergraduate credit is available.
Program: Participants study Native American life and "augment their cultural sensitivity and skills." Projects include work in a social service agency, teaching, contributing on religious missions, etc. The course runs eight weeks—from the end of May to the end of August. Participants do preliminary academic work in March and April and attend a two-day workshop in May.
Requirements: Volunteers must be willing to learn the routine of an office, home, or school, and to spend 40 hours a week helping in any way they are needed.
Age: Minimum 20.
Living Arrangements: Vary from a room in a Native American home to an apartment on a campus or perhaps a room in a dormitory.
Persons with Disabilities: Placements are handled by individual interview and special arrangement.
Finances: Tuition for the course is approximately $700, which covers placement, supervision, and lodging.
Deadline: April 1.
Contact: James M. Mahan, Director, Cultural Immersion Programs.

The Experiment in International Living

P.O. Box 676
Kipling Road
Brattleboro, VT 05302-0676
Phone: (802) 257-7751

Organization: The Experiment is a nonprofit organization dedicated to providing its participants with the knowledge, attitude, and skills to enable them to contribute to international development and understanding.

A participant on the Experiment in International Living's Summer Abroad Program in Kenya receives the gift of a hand-woven basket from her new friends.

Program: The Experiment offers a summer-abroad program for high school students, in which teenagers volunteer for four to six weeks. Activities include work with refugees, work on irrigation projects, providing support for cottage industries, work with the Audubon Society, etc. The Experiment sponsors projects in Australia, Bali, Brazil, Ecuador, France, Germany, Great Britain, Indonesia, Ireland, Italy, Japan, Kenya, Mexico, Saint Vincent, Spain, Switzerland, Thailand, and republics of the former Soviet Union.
Requirements: None.
Age: 14–17.
Living Arrangements: Hotels, dormitories, and homestays.
Persons with Disabilities: The Experiment's policy is nondiscriminatory.
Finances: Fees ranging from $1,600 to $5,600 cover airfare, room, board, in-country travel, orientation, group leaders, and insurance.
Deadline: April 15.
Contact: Summer Abroad.

"My five weeks in Thailand far surpassed my greatest hopes....Getting to know the refugees was especially enlightening, showing me that friendships can develop under any circumstances provided that there is an opportunity for them to form."

Focus

Department of Ophthalmology
Loyola University Medical Center
2160 South First Avenue
Maywood, IL 60153
Phone: (312) 531-3408

Organization: Focus places ophthalmologists in hospitals in Nigeria.

Program: Placements last for a minimum of three weeks.
Requirements: Participants must be certified ophthalmologists.
Finances: Volunteers pay their own travel expenses. Room and board are provided.
Deadline: At least three months are needed to arrange a placement.
Contact: James E. McDonald, President.

Foundation for Field Research

P.O. Box 2010
Alpine, CA 91903
Phone: (619) 445-9264

Organization: The Foundation is a nonprofit organization that sponsors research expeditions by finding volunteers to assist scientists in the field. Founded in 1982, the organization began by using saddle mules to survey large expanses of land for archaeological sites.
Program: Expeditions run from two days to two months and may involve archaeological, botanical, marine biological, or wildlife biological projects. Recently, volunteers assisted in an archaeological excavation of a Roman cemetery in Germany; helped gather sea turtle eggs by night for protection from poachers in Michoacan, Mexico; and worked on a study of the resplendent Quetzal bird, going by foot into the cloud forest of Chiapas, Mexico. In 1991 projects were located in Arizona, California, Connecticut, France, Germany, Ghana, Grenada, Italy, Liberia, Mexico, Montana, New York, Oregon, Sierra Leone, and Spain. Volunteers work five or six days per week, about eight hours each day. The first day of the project is devoted to orientation. Instruction in research techniques is ongoing in the field.

Foundation for Field Research volunteer excavating Native American site in the Southwest.

Requirements: Most volunteers have had no previous experience—"they join to learn by doing, to meet new friends, to have an adventure, and to make an important contribution to research." Scuba diving experience is needed on some of the marine biological expeditions.
Age: Minimum 13.
Living Arrangements: These vary according to project—anything from tent camping to a dormitory-type building to a mid-range hotel. All ex-

peditions are provided with an experienced camp cook. "We have found that participants' time is best spent assisting the researcher, rather than cooking and washing."
Persons with Disabilities: If a participant can maneuver over the terrain of the project they can volunteer.
Finances: Fees vary from project to project. The fee for elephant study in Mali, for example, is $1,672, while the bird census in northern California is $395. These fees or contributions made to the Foundation are tax deductible. Transportation between the assembly point and home (the responsibility of the volunteer) is also deductible. The cost of the contribution covers a grant to the researcher, planning costs, a preparatory booklet, all meals, lodging, transportation during the expedition, and field gear.
Deadline: None.

Foundation for International Youth Exchange

ul. Grzybowska 79
00-844 Warsaw
Poland

Organization: FMWF was founded in the aftermath of Poland's recent political transition. It organizes international workcamps throughout Poland.
Program: Workcamps take place in the summer and last approximately two weeks. Work may involve nature conservation, renovation of historic buildings, or educational tasks.
Requirements: None.
Age: Minimum 18.
Living Arrangements: Volunteers stay in tents, hostels, or school buildings.
Finances: Volunteers pay a placement fee to the national workcamp organization in their own country. Room and board are provided, but the cost of travel to and from the workcamp is the volunteer's responsibility.
Deadline: April 15.
Contact: Volunteers must apply through a national workcamp organization in their own country. For further information, U.S. volunteers must contact the Council on International Educational Exchange (see the organization's listing in this section).

Four Corners School of Outdoor Education

East Route
Monticello, UT 84535
Phone: (800) 525-4456

Organization: This nonprofit institution offers educational field programs in the Four Corners region (the area where Utah, Colorado, Arizona, and New Mexico meet).
Program: Among a wide variety of courses on outdoor survival, the wilderness, and Native American civilization, the Four Corners School offers opportunities to participate in archaeological digs and field surveys.
Requirements: There are physical requirements for some programs, which are rated by level of difficulty.
Age: Minimum 14 without adult supervision.

Living Arrangements: Volunteers live in base camps with primitive facilities. Some programs involve backpacking.
Finances: Courses range from $300 to $1,400, including room and board, equipment, supplies, and insurance.
Deadline: None.
Contact: Janet Ross, Director.

Fourth World Movement

7600 Willow Hill Drive
Landover, MD 20785
Phone: (301) 336-9489

Organization: Founded in 1957, the Movement runs cultural and educational projects in partnership with extremely poor families in 22 countries on five continents based on the conviction: "Wherever men and women are condemned to live in extreme poverty, human rights are violated. It is our solemn duty to come together to ensure that they are respected."
Program: The Movement holds a number of two-week summer workcamps (from June through September). Work/information camps are held for 10 days during the summer. Work may involve construction, cooking, gardening, library work, typing, or packaging greeting cards. Evenings are reserved for films and discussions on extreme poverty. Participants also meet and work with long-term volunteers who have worked in very poor areas. Most workcamps are held at the Movement's international center near Paris. Some are also offered in Belgium, Germany, Great Britain, the Netherlands, and Switzerland.
Requirements: Participants must be in good health.
Age: Minimum 18 for regular workcamps. Special workcamps are offered at a youth center for participants of 16 and 17 years.
Living Arrangements: Participants share cabins or tents and eat together.
Finances: Housing is provided. participants are asked to contribute to the costs of groceries and to pay their own travel expenses and health insurance.
Deadline: Two weeks before camp.
Contact: For regular workcamps in France, contact the Fourth World Movement at the address above. For teenage workcamps or workcamps in other European countries, contact the Movement at 107 avenue du G. Leclerc, 95480 Pierrelaye, France.

"Doing manual labor was a show of solidarity with the poor. I felt I'd been missing something very basic by not working with my hands."

"I realized that the poor are to be respected in their struggle against the denial of human rights. They hold the key to their own freedom, if anyone would listen to them."

Friends Weekend Workcamps

1515 Cherry Street
Philadelphia, PA 19102
Phone: (215) 241-7236

Organization: Weekend Workcamps provides opportunities for people of different backgrounds to live, learn, and work together.
Program: Groups of up to 18 volun-

teers spend a weekend together, from Friday supper to Sunday afternoon, working and socializing. Most of the work is done on Saturday; it may involve painting or plastering in a neighborhood home, working with senior citizens, children, or the handicapped. In August there is a two-week workcamp for international volunteers. Longer-term volunteers are welcome.
Requirements: No special skills are necessary.
Age: Minimum 15; anyone under 18 must have written parental consent.
Living Arrangements: Volunteers stay in a row house, where they sleep on mattresses on the floor.
Finances: Participants pay $35 to cover the cost of room and board and insurance.
Deadline: None. First come, first served. There are two weekend workcamps per month from October to May.
Contact: Michael Van Hoy or Kathryn Maleney.

Frontiers Foundation/ Operation Beaver

2615 Danforth Avenue, Suite 203
Toronto, Ontario, Canada M4C 1L6
Phone: (416) 690-3930

Organization: Frontiers works in rural communities in some of the remotest regions of Canada to build and renovate homes, schools, churches, and community centers.
Program: Volunteers from all over the world come together for 12 weeks (June–August), or for up to 18 months to work on Foundation-sponsored projects in participating communities.
Requirements: No special qualifications are required, but carpentry, plumbing, electrical, or general residential construction/renovation skills are an asset. "Our prime concerns are honesty, sincerity, and an open mind."
Age: Minimum 18.
Living Arrangements: Volunteers live together in community centers, private houses, or schools.
Persons with Disabilities: Application is open to volunteers with limited disabilities.
Finances: Travel to and from the project site and living expenses during the project are paid by Operation Beaver.
Deadline: February 15.
Contact: Marco Guzman, Program Coordinator

"What I primarily gained from the summer was a greatly increased understanding of people, of living together, of poverty and of the strength of the human spirit."

Genctur Tourism and Travel

Yerebatan Caddesi 15/3
34410 Sultanahmet
Istanbul
Turkey

Organization: Genctur is the Turkish youth travel bureau. Among other activities, it organizes workcamps throughout Turkey.

Program: Workcamps operate for two weeks at a time from June to October. In 1987, there were 12 camps in four provinces. Volunteers do manual labor (like painting schools, digging sewers, building bridges, or digging water channels). The aim of the camps is "to do a job which benefits all the villagers and fulfills a basic need." The work is not the only important part of the camp—"just as important is the contact we make with the villagers." An optional post-camp holiday by the sea can be arranged by Genctur.
Requirements: None.
Age: 18–35.
Living Arrangements: Volunteers live together in a public building, usually a school. "You will live under the same conditions as the people in the village, eat the same way they do...and you will also join them in their social activities such as weddings, circumcisions, and religious feasts."
Finances: Volunteers pay a placement fee to the national workcamp organization in their own country. Room and board are provided, but the cost of travel to and from the workcamp is the volunteer's responsibility.
Deadline: April 15.
Contact: Volunteers must apply through a national workcamp organization in their own country. For further information, U.S. volunteers must contact either the Council on International Educational Exchange or Volunteers for Peace (see these organizations' listings in this section).

Genesis II

Apartado 10303
1000 San José
Costa Rica
Phone: (506) 250271

Organization: Genesis II owns an expanse of tropical cloudforest at the 2360 meter level in the Talamanca Mountains of central Costa Rica. From its inception it has been intended and operated as a preserve for academic research and recreational (non-hunting) pleasure. Within its 95 acres can be found up to 120 species of birds plus many types of ferns, orchids, and fungi, as well as its major plant, the giant white oak.
Program: Volunteers are asked to make a minimum commitment of six weeks. They work for the first 30 days and have the remaining 12 days off. Tasks include construction, landscaping, reforestation, and trail making and maintenance.
Requirements: None, but preference is given to those with previous volunteer or outdoor experience and studies in ecology, conservation, etc.
Age: Minimum 21.
Living Arrangements: Volunteers live in cabins with bunk beds and solar lighting. All eat together in the main house.
Finances: Volunteers are asked to make a minimum contribution of US$75 a week, to cover room, board, and laundry facilities.
Deadline: The program operates all year except in December. Each six-week unit is limited to seven volunteers and is closed when full.
Contact: Steve Friedman.

"Actively contributing to the conservation of a truly endangered environment is satisfying beyond description. I can at last be content, at least temporarily, that I have directly helped a worthwhile and essential project."

Global Volunteers

375 East Little Canada Road
St. Paul, MN 55117
Phone: (800) 487-1074

Organization: Global Volunteers is a nonprofit organization with one- to three-week volunteer work/learning programs in communities in Africa, Asia, the Caribbean, Central America, Eastern Europe, North America, and the South Pacific.
Program: Teams of 8 to 12 volunteers live and work in rural communities and participate in economic and human development projects. Projects take place in Guatemala, Indonesia, Jamaica, Mexico, the Mississippi Delta, Poland, Tanzania, and Tonga, and include construction of schools and clinics, tutoring, health care, and business planning.
Requirements: None.
Age: Minimum 18 without a guardian.
Living Arrangements: Volunteers live together in a village building.
Persons with Disabilities: Global Volunteers will accept volunteers of any background.
Finances: Tax-deductible fees range from $525 to $1,825 (plus airfare) and cover training materials, ground transportation, hotel rooms, village lodging and meals, and project expenses.
Deadline: Allow four weeks to process visas, etc.

Gruppo Volontari della Svizzera Italiana

Casella postale 12
6517 Arbedo
Switzerland
Phone (41-92) 29 13 37

Organizaton: GVSI is a nonprofit workcamp organization based in the Italian-speaking region of Switzerland.
Program: GVSI organizes workcamps in Europe—Switzerland in particular—as well as in Honduras and Mexico. Workcamps focus on community service and recreation.
Requirements: Volunteers should be able to speak French or Italian.
Age: Minimum 18.
Living Arrangements: Arrangements vary; homestays are possible.
Finances: Room and board provided.
Deadline: None.
Contact: Mari Federico, Coordinatore.

Heifer Project International Learning and Livestock Center

Route 2, Box 33
Perryville, AR 72126
Phone: (501) 889-5124

Organization: Founded in 1944 Heifer Project International supplies livestock and related agricultural services to low-income families throughout the world. Each recipient passes on offspring to others in need. The Learning and Livestock Center is a 1,200 acre ranch, 40 miles west of Little Rock. The center raises livestock for production, shipping, and training. A conference center offers a wide variety of educational programming. Livestock includes cattle, sheep, draft animals, goats, swine, rabbits, poultry, fish, and bees.

Program: Volunteers assist the staff in the daily operation of the ranch. Tasks include caring for the livestock, maintenance, construction, office work, gardening, and landscaping. Volunteers may serve for one to eight weeks.

Requirements: No special skills are required. "Maturity, flexibility, a positive attitude, and a desire to live in a rural area are essential."

Age: Minimum 18.

Living Arrangements: Some volunteers live together in a house on the ranch and share rooms with one or two others; other volunteers live in rental housing near the center. Noon meals are served on weekdays in the cafeteria, other meals are the responsibility of the volunteers.

Persons with Disabilities: Applications are reviewed on a case by case basis. Lodgings are wheelchair accessible.

Finances: Room and board are provided. A modest stipend may be available.

Deadline: At least two months in advance of desired starting volunteering date.

Contact: Arlene Musselman, Volunteer Coordinator.

Human Service Alliance

3983 Old Greensboro Road
Winston-Salem, NC 27101
Phone: (919) 761-8745

Organization: HSA is a nonprofit human service organization that provides respite care for developmentally disabled persons, care for the terminally ill, mediation (conflict resolution), and health and wellness support at its Care for the Terminally Ill Center. The Center offers a home-like setting where the guests live out their lives in a loving and supportive environment.

Program: Every aspect of the Center's operation is staffed by volunteers, so you can contribute in any number of ways. One role is caring directly for the guests, much as a loving family member would: keeping them company, helping with their grooming, reading to them, or simply holding hands. In addition to direct care, there are other equally important functions like cooking, housekeeping, gardening and grounds maintenance, typing, computer work, and much more. Both short- and long-term volunteers are needed.

Requirements: No prior special training is needed. Training is provided by HSA.

Age: Volunteers can be any age.

Living Arrangements: There are a number of comfortable rooms for full-time, live-in volunteers. During free time, Winston-Salem offers a wide variety of activities.

Persons with Disabilities: Persons with disabilities are encouraged to apply.

Finances: Volunteers are provided with room and board.
Deadline: None.
Contact: Christa Danziger, Volunteer Team.

Institute of Cultural Affairs

4750 North Sheridan Road
Chicago, IL 60640
Phone: (312) 769-6363

Organization: ICA is a private, nonprofit organization concerned with the human element in world development. Formerly the research division of the Ecumenical Institute, it has been operating since 1973, designing and applying methods of human development in communities and organizations. Since 1989, national ICAs have cooperated through ICA International, Brussels. ICA's research, demonstration, training, and consultative programs are problem-solving and action-oriented, using methods of community and organizational transformation.

Program: ICA Chicago has five volunteer work-study programs. "The Space Between" is conducted in conjunction with ICA Peru, ICA Guatemala, and ICA Mexico. It offers a two- to four-week experience of working and interacting with local people while living with a village family. "The International Camp for Community Activists" is a work-study experience conducted in New York and concluded with a trip to a human development project in Portugal. "The Village Volunteer Program" is run through ICA International in Brussels. A limited number of volunteers are accepted in national ICAs on the basis of need in that country. They work as part of a team and live in the community under similar conditions to those they serve and receive training or orientation in the U.S. or Brussels. "Leadership Options" is a 16-day experience in a learning community exploring the depressed, underdeveloped community of uptown Chicago, where 84 different languages are spoken. Persons considering careers in the volunteer and nonprofit sectors can learn firsthand about the challenges faced and methods to meet them. Resources include the urban service agency network as well as resident ICA staff. "Residential Urban Internships" range from three to nine months to fit the needs of the intern, but usually involve volunteer work with ICA or other Chicago agencies while doing special study or research in Chicago either independently or under the supervision of ICA staff.

Requirements: Specific requirements vary from program to program, but ICA is "looking for people who are mature enough to interact creatively."

Age: At least two years of college are recommended, but graduate students, career switchers, and retirees will all find an appropriate challenge.

Living Arrangements: Volunteers live in staff housing, training centers, or with arranged families, depending on the location.

Finances: Volunteers must be self-supporting while on assignment as well as cover the costs of their training, orientation, travel, room, and board. ICA covers expenses of project-related work only.

Deadline: Varies.
Contact: Audrey Ayres or George Packard.

Instituto de la Juventud

Jose Ortega y Gasset 71
28006 Madrid
Spain

Organization: The Instituto is an agency of the Spanish government which organizes Voluntary service opportunities in Spain.
Program: The Instituto organizes hundreds of workcamps throughout Spain each summer, each lasting about two weeks. Volunteers may be involved in archaeological digs, environmental work, construction, or other projects. Workcamps in Spain differ from those in other countries in that only two or three foreigners are placed on each project, the rest of the participants being Spanish. For this reason, foreign volunteers must be flexible in accepting assignments.
Requirements: Participants must have a good working knowledge of Spanish.
Age: Minimum 18.
Living Arrangements: Volunteers live in tents, youth hostels, and schools, depending on the site.
Finances: Volunteers pay a placement fee to the national workcamp organization in their own country. Room and board are provided, but the cost of travel to and from the workcamp is the volunteer's responsibility.
Deadline: April 15.
Contact: Volunteers must apply through a national workcamp organization in their own country. For further information, U.S. volunteers must contact either the Council on International Educational Exchange or Volunteers for Peace (see these organizations' listings in this section).

International Association of Dental Students

c/o Executive Director
Fédération Dentaire Internationale
64 Wimpole Street
London W1M 8AL
United Kingdom

Organization: IADS was founded in Copenhagen in 1951. It aims to stimulate the interest of dental students in the advancement of the science and art of dentistry, while promoting cultural and social contact between dental students and dental student organizations throughout the world. It also aims to represent dental students at the international level.
Program: IADS's Voluntary Work Abroad Program sends students and young practitioners to countries that need aid. Volunteers work for three weeks to three months. Thus far, the program is operative in Africa, with plans to expand to other regions.
Requirements: Volunteers must be dental students or professionals.
Finances: IADS attempts as much as possible to arrange free room and board for volunteers.
Deadline: None.
Contact: Marcel Cucu, International Exchange Officer of IADS, Postiljonsgatan 11, 431 66 Mölndal, Sweden.

International Christian Youth Exchange

Short-Term Programs
134 West 26th Street
New York, NY 10001
Phone: (212) 206-7307

Organization: ICYE is an international, intercultural organization composed of autonomous national committees in 32 countries. In the U.S., ICYE is divided into volunteer regional teams which plan and carry out programs for U.S. exchangees going abroad, exchangees spending their year in the U.S., and host families. The national program staff is based in New York City, with an area office in Northern California. ICYE began as a bilateral exchange program with Germany in 1949, and in 1957 branched out to include other countries.

Program: Young people spend four to six weeks as summer volunteers involved in international workcamps in one of a number of projects spanning Africa, Asia, Europe, and Latin America. Past projects include rehabilitation of a school and medical clinic in a rural fishing village in Ghana; service in the field of women's health care, with opportunities for work in abuse centers, local clinics, prenatal care delivery, and counseling centers in Latin America; working on national park restoration in France; or other possibilities. Predeparture preparation is complemented by in-country orientation and evaluation conferences; seminars and cultural events as well as study tours complete the program.

Requirements: "The adjustments required in an international exchange experience demand adaptability, resourcefulness, maturity, integrity, common sense, convictions, and stability."

Age: 16–35.

Living Arrangements: Volunteers live with local families or are housed in schools, clinics, or other independent living situations.

Persons with Disabilities: All projects are open to persons with physical disabilities.

Finances: Participation fees cover room, board, international travel, insurance, orientation, evaluation, and conferences, and ranges from $250 to $2,600. Some scholarship aid is available for volunteers.

Deadline: Applications reviewed on a space-available basis, through departure date.

Contact: Workcamps Department.

International Voluntary Service

122 Great Victoria Street
Belfast, BT2 7BG
Northern Ireland

Organization: IVS is part of the Service Civil International network involved in international workcamps.

Program: Workcamps last for two to three weeks and generally involve social work, community work, construction, conservation, and ecology projects. Most opportunities occur between June and September.

Requirements: No special skills are required.

Age: Minimum 18.
Living Arrangements: Volunteers live in some form of group living arrangement.
Persons with Disabilities: Persons with disabilities are encouraged to apply.
Finances: Volunteers pay a placement fee to the national workcamp organization in their own country. Room and board are provided, but the cost of travel to and from the workcamp is the volunteer's responsibility.
Deadline: None, but the earlier the better.
Contact: Volunteers must apply through a national workcamp organization in their own country. For further information, U.S. volunteers must contact Service Civil International—International Voluntary Service (see the organization's listings in this section).

Internationale Begegnung Gemeinschaftsdiensten

Schlosserstrasse 28
2000 Stuttgart 1
Germany

Organization: IBG is a long-standing service organization offering a variety of workcamps in Germany and Switzerland. IBG has recently begun working with workcamp organizations in the eastern part of Germany.
Program: IBG's workcamps take place during the summer and last approximately two weeks. Projects include environmental protection, restoration, and park maintenance.
Requirements: Some workcamps require a knowledge of German.
Age: Minimum 18.
Living Arrangements: Vary.
Finances: Volunteers pay a placement fee to the national workcamp organization in their own country. Room and board are provided, but the cost of travel to and from the workcamp is the volunteer's responsibility.
Deadline: April 15.
Contact: Volunteers must apply through a national workcamp organization in their own country. For further information, U.S. volunteers must contact the Council on International Educational Exchange (see the organization's listing in this section).

Internationale Jugendgemeinschaftsdienste

Kaiserstrasse 43
5300 Bonn 1
Germany

Program: IJGD sponsors three- to four-week workcamps during Easter vacation and from June to October, mainly in the social/cultural/historical sphere, environmental protection, and city fringe recreation activities. Volunteers work approximately six hours per day.
Requirements: Some workcamps require a knowledge of German.
Age: 16–25.
Finances: Volunteers pay a placement fee to the national workcamp organization in their own country. Room and board are provided, but the cost of travel to and from the

workcamp is the volunteer's responsibility.
Deadline: April 15.
Contact: Volunteers must apply through a national workcamp organization in their own country. For further information, U.S. volunteers must contact either the Council on International Educational Exchange or Volunteers for Peace (see these organizations' listing in this section).

"It was truly wonderful to meet people from such varied backgrounds...even with such varied interests and opinions, we got along great and became a cohesive group."

Involvement Volunteers

P.O. Box 218
Port Melbourne, Victoria 3207
Australia
Phone: (61-3) 646 5504

Organization: Involvement Volunteers is a nonprofit organization which finds suitable positions for volunteers with community-based organizations in all states of Australia, California, Fiji, Germany, India, and Thailand.
Program: Volunteers spend 2 to 12 weeks involved in activities related to conservation, construction, social service, and specific education or research programs in both rural and urban areas.
Requirements: Many positions only require a desire to get "dirty fingers" and a willingness to share their abilities with other people. Volunteers with special skills are matched with a suitable project.
Age: Minimum 17.
Living Arrangements: Depending on the project, volunteers may be housed with farmers' families, in sheep shearers' quarters, in tents, in villages or in cities.
Persons with Disabilities: Providing the project is suitable, persons with disabilities may apply. An understanding of spoken English is necessary.
Finances: There is a placement fee of AUS$300. Room and board are generally provided, but some situations can require a contribution toward project costs. Volunteers meet all travel expenses.
Deadline: None. Positions are available all year round, but allow time to be placed.
Contact: Ellen Linsley, Involvement Corps, 15515 Sunset Boulevard, Suite 108, Pacific Palisades, CA 90272; (213) 459-1022.

Israel Department of Antiquities and Museums

P.O. Box 586
Jerusalem 91004, Israel
Phone: (972-2) 278602

Organization: This branch of the Israeli government publishes a booklet each year called *Archaeological Excavations* which lists ongoing survey projects and excavation sites.
Program: Excavations take place throughout the year, but the main season for activity is June to September. Volunteers are needed to dig, clean pottery shards, and more; the work is difficult and requires that

volunteers be in good physical condition. Volunteers must commit themselves to at least one week of work; some digs require more time. Volunteers may sleep in the field in sleeping bags or in rooms in hostels or kibbutzim. Room and board may be provided, but more often there's a small charge for food and accommodation. Some expeditions offer credit from sponsoring institutions.
Persons with Disabilities: The work is extremely strenuous, hard physical labor at sites that sometimes have no direct access other than by hiking or climbing. It is recommended that those who have impaired mobility not participate in such excavations.
Contact: The various excavations listed in the booklet must be contacted directly. Copies of the booklet are available from the Israel Government Tourist Office in New York (350 Fifth Avenue, New York, NY 10118), or from Israel's embassies and consulates.

Jeunesse et Reconstruction

10, rue de Trevisse
75009 Paris
France

Program: The organization operates workcamps during the summer months. Volunteers are generally involved in construction, refurbishing, or ecology projects.
Requirements: No special skills are required.
Age: Minimum 18.
Living Arrangements: Volunteers live in shared accommodations which vary depending on the project.

Finances: Volunteers pay a placement fee to the national workcamp organization in their own country. Room and board are provided, but the cost of travel to and from the workcamp is the volunteer's responsibility.
Deadline: April 15.
Contact: Volunteers must apply through a national workcamp organization in their own country. For further information, U.S. volunteers should contact either the Council on International Educational Exchange or Volunteers for Peace (see these organizations' listings in this section).

Joint Assistance Centre

H-65, South Extension-1
New Delhi-110 049
India
Phone: (91-11) 697986

Organization: JAC is a small voluntary service organization headquartered in New Delhi. JAC mainly works in liaison with other groups in India on projects of various types.
Program: Volunteers generally work from four weeks to six months. Projects include teaching, construction, editing newsletters and promotional material, social service, and environmental conservation.
Requirements: Volunteers must refrain from smoking, drinking, and eating nonvegetarian food.
Age: Minimum 18.
Living Arrangements: Volunteers sleep on a floor, sharing kitchen and bath facilities. At times there is no electricity but the water is safe.
Persons with Disabilities: Persons

with disabilities can participate as long as they can handle local transportation.
Finances: Volunteers pay a $20 registration fee plus $120 a month, which includes room and board.
Deadline: None.
Contact: Address above (include three International Reply Coupons), or Friends of JAC in the Americas, c/o K. Gopalan, P.O. Box 14481, Santa Rosa, CA 95402.

Kibbutz Aliya

27 West 20th Street
New York, NY 10011
Phone: (212) 255-1338

Organization: Kibbutz Aliya represents Israel's kibbutz movement in North America. It screens and places volunteers in kibbutzim-cooperative communities all over Israel.
Program: Volunteers serve a minimum of one month and may extend their stay with the permission of the kibbutz. "It takes at least a month to become accustomed to the different lifestyles and working conditions and to become acquainted with the kibbutz members and people from other parts of the world." Work is generally in the agricultural branches of the kibbutz but may be in the industrial or service branch instead. Opportunities exist year round but in the summer it may take a bit more time to place volunteers than at other times of the year. Work on the kibbutz means putting in six to eight hours a day, six days a week.
Requirements: Volunteers must be in good physical condition and willing to work shoulder-to-shoulder with their Israeli counterparts. All prospective participants are interviewed by a representative of Kibbutz Aliya before being certified. References are necessary.
Age: 18–35. Married couples without children are eligible for the program.
Living Arrangements: Volunteers share dorm-style accommodations with one or two others.
Finances: There's a $75 registration fee and a minimum insurance fee of $50. Room and board, laundry services, and a small personal allowance are provided; participants pay their own travel costs to and from Israel.
Deadline: None.

"I had a great time... The kibbutz was very good to me, and my experiences were varied, fun, and useful. I gained a lot of confidence from working hard on the kibbutz, and staying six months gave me insight into kibbutz life."

Koinonia Partners

Route 2, Dawson Road
Americus, GA 31709
Phone: (912) 924-0391

Organization: In 1942 two couples, the Jordans and the Englands, started an experiment in Christian living in southwest Georgia, giving it a name that is Greek for fellowship. They had two purposes: first, "to live in community and bear witness to Christian teachings" and second, to assist local farmers. The community continues and now Koinonia Partners sponsors a housing program whereby homes are built and sold at cost with no-in-

terest mortgages. It also sponsors an educational program for children and adults in Sumter County, operates a mail-order food business, has a large garden, and farms 700 acres of land.
Program: Volunteers live with the community for a three-month period from March to May, June to August or September to December. Those who can only get away for one month may arrange to spend the month of January in the community. (In 1992, Koinonia Partner's Jubilee Year, volunteer programs will operate only in January and the fall.) Volunteers may be assigned any number of tasks; processing and shipping pecan orders, office work, weeding the garden, pruning the vineyard, repairing automobiles, etc. "Most of our work may not be stimulating intellectually, but we hope you'll find satisfaction in greeting the end of the day with a feeling that you've done an important-to-the-whole job, even if it is monotonous!" There may also be opportunities for volunteers to work with neighbors in tutoring programs. Two or three hours of the workday is spent in study and/or discussion.
Requirements: No special skills are required; a willingness to work wherever needed is important. "Although someone coming to be with us as a volunteer need not be Christian, it is important that prospective volunteers have a sincere desire to explore with us the meaning of Christian discipleship."
Living Arrangements: Room and board are provided in households with members of the community.
Finances: Living expenses are provided.

Deadline: Indicated on application form.
Contact: Volunteer Coordinator.

L'Arche Mobile

151 South Ann Street
Mobile, AL 36604
Phone: (205) 438-2094

Organization: L'Arche Mobile, an ecumenical Christian community where mentally disabled people live together as a family with non-disabled people, is a member of the International Federation of L'Arche, begun in France in 1964.
Program: L'Arche Mobile creates a homelike environment for persons with mental disabilities. Most residents come from institutions where they have had little contact with their own families. A Day/Work Program focuses on the needs and abilities of each person. Typical projects include activities such as arts and crafts, yard work, and baking. Each person's schedule combines exercise with accomplishing goals in the workplace.
Requirements: None.
Age: Minimum 18.
Living Arrangements: Volunteers live in private rooms, with a separate apartment available for days off.
Persons with Disabilities: Persons with disabilities are accepted. Housing is accessible.
Finances: Volunteers receive room, board, insurance, and, after the first month, $325 a month.
Deadline: None.
Contact: Martin E. O'Malley, Director.

La Sabranenque

Centre Internationale
rue de la Tour de l'Oume
30290 Saint Victor la Coste
France
Phone: (33) 66 50 05 05

Organization: La Sabranenque is a nonprofit organization aimed at the preservation of rural habitats through practical projects and programs offering discovery of village life and work.
Program: Workcamps are conducted during the summer, and run from two weeks to three months. Volunteers participate in ongoing restoration projects on typical structures in villages using traditional techniques. Project sites are in France and Italy.
Requirements: No experience or languages are required.
Age: Minimum 18.
Living Arrangements: Participants live in rooms for two in restored stone houses.
Persons with Disabilities: There are no restrictions, but work is physically demanding and pathways are rough.
Finances: The fee for the two-week program is approximately $490, covering room, board, and insurance.
Deadline: None.
Contact: Jacqueline Simon, 217 High Park Boulevard, Buffalo, NY 14226; (716) 836-8698.

"My summer experience at la Sabranenque was truly one of the best I've ever had. I enjoyed the work environment and the communal atmosphere as much as the unique opportunity to discover the history and culture of the Provençal region."

La Sabranenque volunteers engaged in the reconstruction of a small medieval bridge near the village of Collias in southern France.

The Lisle Fellowship

433 West Sterns Road
Temperance, MI 48182
Phone: (313) 847-7126

Organization: The Lisle Fellowship is an intercultural education agency which, in its over 50 years of existence, has sponsored hundreds of programs in 15 countries.
Program: Lisle sponsors programs usually of three to four weeks. It offers programs in India in cooperation with the Gandhi Peace Foundation; in Bali in cooperation with the Candi Dasa Ashram; in Mexico in cooperation with CIRIMEX; and in Japan in cooperation with the Sapporo International Communications Plaza. It also offers an Elderhostel program in cross-cultural sharing at the University of Toledo in Ohio. All programs build people to people understanding and appreciation of diverse cultures, religions, and ways of life. The purpose of these programs is to develop a view of the world which creates lasting peace and survival.
Requirements: Participants should be able to share in group life, be sensitive to others, be alert to cultural clues, and have a concern for the well-being of others.
Age: Minimum 18; Elderhostel participants must be 60.
Living Arrangements: Participants live in accommodations comparable to those of the inhabitants of the community in which they work. Usual housing is spartan but complete. Homestays are usually included in each program.
Persons with Disabilities: All persons who can accommodate to the program's travel and lodging requirements are welcome.
Finances: Fees range from $490 to $2,200, plus airfare. The Elderhostel program costs approximately $270.
Deadline: Depends upon the individual program; approximately three months in advance.
Contact: Mark B. Kinney, President.

Los Niños

9765 Marconi Drive, Suite 105
San Ysidro, CA 92173
Phone: (619) 661-6912

Organization: Founded in 1974, Los Niños is a nonprofit organization providing community development services in the areas of literacy, early education, health, and nutrition. Also provided is the educating of U.S. volunteers about development and Mexico.
Program: Los Niños works with orphanages and communities in the Mexican border cities of Mexicali and Tijuana. Short-term volunteers may attend educational workshops for a weekend to 10 days during the period from October to May, or the summer program from July to August. Most short-term volunteers are high school and college students; long-term volunteers assist in literacy, early education, nutrition, and agricultural programs.
Requirements: A minimum of conversational Spanish is required.
Age: High school students are eligible for short-term programs; long-term volunteers must be 18.

Living Arrangements: Volunteers live in Tijuana in a community living situation. Everyone shares housekeeping tasks.
Persons with Disabilities: Everyone is welcome to apply.
Finances: There's a required fee for weekend and summer programs to cover room and board; volunteers who serve for one year or more receive free room and board.
Deadline: None.
Contact: Roque Barros, Executive Director.

"Los Niños allowed me to learn about Mexican culture and develop my Spanish skills while learning about the border reality."

Macon Program for Progress

38 1/2 East Main Street
P.O. Box 700
Franklin, NC 28734
Phone: (704) 524-4471

Organization: This community action agency works to alleviate the causes and conditions of poverty by mobilizing local, state, and federal resources.
Program: Many volunteers are used on various part-time projects, but a full-time opportunity is the one-week Volunteer House Project. Other opportunities include working with children and/or the elderly.
Requirements: Construction skills are helpful, but not necessary.
Age: Minimum 16.
Living Arrangements: Accommodation information is provided on request.
Finances: Volunteers must pay their own travel and lodging expenses. Lunch and dinner are provided for participants of the Volunteer House Project.
Deadline: August 15.
Contact: Mary Ann Sloan, Executive Director or Rick Norton, Housing Coordinator.

Malta Youth Hostels Association

17, Triq Tal-Borg
Pawla, Malta
Phone (356) 239361

Organization: MYHA promotes international understanding by providing inexpensive accommodation in youth hostels.
Program: Volunteers are needed to administer, maintain, and repair youth hostels or work on hostel-related projects in Malta (three hours a day, seven days a week).
Requirements: None.
Age: 16–50.
Living Arrangements: Volunteers live in youth hostels.
Persons with Disabilities: The youth hostels have no special facilities.
Finances: Volunteers receive free accommodations and breakfast.
Deadline: Normally three months before the start of work (sessions begin on the 1st and 15th of each month). Apply as early as possible for the high season.
Contact: The W.S. Organizer (enclose two International Reply Coupons).

Mellemfolkeligt Samvirke

Borgergade 10-14
1300 Copenhagen K
Denmark

Organization: Mellemfolkeligt Samvirke is the Danish Association for International Cooperation. The organization operates the Danish Volunteer Service, which sends volunteers to Third World countries; International Youth Exchange, which organizes workcamps; and an information department which publishes books and magazines on international development.
Program: Workcamps are organized in Denmark, Greenland, and on the Faroe Islands. The projects include construction of playgrounds, nature conservation, and restoration.
Requirements: No special skills are needed, except in Greenland where some working experience in a trade is required.
Age: Minimum 18.
Persons with Disabilities: Some camps are open to persons with disabilities.
Finances: Volunteers pay a placement fee to the national workcamp organization in their own country. Room and board are provided, but the cost of travel to and from the workcamp is the volunteer's responsibility.
Deadline: April 15.
Contact: Volunteers must apply through a national workcamp organization in their own country. For further information, U.S. volunteers should contact either the Council on International Educational Exchange or Volunteers for Peace (see these organizations' listings in this section).

Mennonite Central Committee

21 South 12th Street
Box M
Akron, PA 17501-0500
Phone: (717) 859-1151

Organization: MCC is the cooperative relief and service agency of North American Mennonite and Brethren in Christ church conferences.
Program: In addition to long-term service work, MCC offers short-term programs especially for young people. These include Sharing With Appalachian People (SWAP), a week-long home-repair program; Urban Community Development Summer Service Program for college-age minority youth; Canada Summer Service; the Native Gardening Program, in which volunteers garden in Native American communities throughout Canada; Denver Opportunity for Outreach and Reflection (DOOR); and the Mennonite Disaster Service.
Requirements: None.
Age: High school and college students.
Living Arrangements: These vary but "can be quite rustic."
Persons with Disabilities: Since 1986 MCC has had a project to integrate persons with disabilities as volunteers into its programs.
Finances: Room and board and in some cases a stipend are provided.
Deadline: Varies.
Contact: Personnel Services.

Mir Initiative

P.O. Box 28183
Washington, DC 20038-8183
Phone: (202) 857-8037

Organization: In conjunction with the Baikal Foundation, a Russian non-governmental organization, Mir Initiative administers The Cooperation Project, sending students and volunteers from around the world to the Lake Baikal region of Siberia.
Program: Workcamps run for two to three weeks during the summer. Participants choose from a range of projects including construction and ecological work.
Requirements: Knowledge of Russian is helpful but not required.
Age: None.
Living Arrangements: Participants share two-person rooms at a campsite on the edge of the Bratsk Reservoir.
Persons with Disabilities: Persons with disabilities are encouraged to apply.
Finances: The program costs $250, which includes room, board, in-country transportation, and emergency medical care.
Deadline: May 1.
Contact: Alexandra Taymar, Director.

Mobility International/USA

P.O. Box 3551
Eugene, OR 97403
Phone: (503) 343-1284

Organization: MIUSA promotes the integration of people with disabilities into international exchange, community service, and travel. As part of its efforts, the organization publishes a quarterly newsletter called *Over the Rainbow* and a book called *A World of Options for the 90s: A Guide to International Educational Exchange, Community Service, and Travel for Persons with Disabilities.*
Program: MIUSA sponsors international exchange programs for three to four weeks during the summer. Each of these exchange programs includes a workcamp component in which people with and without disabilities from around the world work together on community projects. In past years, projects have involved making a national forest accessible by wheelchair, painting, and building ramps. Homestays are included in the program. MIUSA also helps people with disabilities who want to participate in other workcamp programs to find the right camp and sponsors exchange programs including voluntary service in other countries. Programs vary yearly. Contact MIUSA for current information.
Requirements: All applicants should be interested in disability issues. Both able-bodied and disabled people are encouraged to apply.
Age: Minimum 18; other age limits vary according to the program.
Living Arrangements: These vary but are always as wheelchair-accessible as possible.
Persons with Disabilities: It is MIUSA's purpose to promote international opportunities for persons with disabilities. The organization actively recruits and encourages both disabled and nondisabled persons for its programs which are fully integrated. MIUSA also advocates in-

volvement for persons with disabilities in all international organizations.
Finances: Vary.
Deadline: Varies.
Contact: Susan Sygall, Director.

"When I volunteered in Costa Rica working with deaf children, I showed them that I, a deaf person, can do anything, including travel to another country."

National Trust for Places of Natural Beauty and Historic Interest

P.O. Box 12
Westbury, WILTS
BA13 4NA England
Phone: (44-373) 826826

Organization: This nonprofit organization, which conserves landscapes and famous homes, is England's largest conservation charity.
Project: Volunteers are needed year-round for projects lasting one to two weeks. Activities include archaeology, bio-surveys, and construction.
Requirements: None.
Age: Minimum 17.
Living Arrangements: Base camps with bunks and showers; separate dorms for men and women.
Persons with Disabilities: In 1992 new projects will be developed for persons with disabilities.
Finances: A fee of £34 per week covers room and board.
Deadline: None.
Contact: Beryl Sims.

National Venceremos Brigade

P.O. Box 673
New York, NY 10035
Phone: (212) 246-3811, ext. 503

Organization: The National Venceremos Brigade is a U.S.-based organization whose aim is to support the Cuban Revolution and improve U.S. relations with Cuba. The Venceremos Brigade organizes groups of U.S. citizens to visit the island for tours conducted by the Cuban government.
Program: In the course of these tours, participants spend several days performing volunteer work in construction and farming. Groups are usually organized for the spring.
Requirements: Good health and a willingness to respect the customs and laws of Cuba. Participants must be U.S. citizens with a valid passport.
Age: Minimum 18.
Living Arrangements: In dormitories separated according to gender.
Persons with Disabilities: Persons with disabilities are encouraged to participate.
Finances: Total cost comes to around $1000, including international transportation, room, and board.
Deadline: None.
Contact: Recruitment Coordinator.

National Venceremos Brigade volunteers laying a concrete foundation in Havana Province, Cuba.

Nothelfergemeinschaft der Freunde

Auf der Körnerwiese 5
D-6000 Frankfurt/Main 1
Germany
Phone: (49-69) 599557

Organization: The name of the organization means "association of friends." It is involved in organizing workcamps in Germany and abroad.
Program: Workcamps are held at Easter and during the summer for three or four weeks. Volunteers from all over the world work in regions hit by catastrophe or in distressed areas. They may help construct a building for the handicapped, the elderly, or other people in need or counsel people involved in a disaster.
Requirements: No special skills are required.
Age: 16–25.
Finances: Volunteers pay an initial fee of DM 70; DM 25 is reimbursed at the end of camp; room and board are provided.
Deadline: May 31.
Contact: Paul Krahe, President.

Operation Crossroads Africa

475 Riveside Drive, Suite 242
New York, NY 10115
Phone: (212) 870-2106

Organization: Since 1957, OCA has conducted programs in Africa and the Caribbean aimed at broadening the scope of international understanding and cooperation while making a tangible contribution to the process of development.
Program: Participants on the Africa

program spend seven weeks living and working with communities on development projects which typically involve physical labor several hours each day. Programs are designed to provide maximum interaction. Tentative project sites are: Botswana, Côte d'Ivoire, Gambia, Kenya, Lesotho, Senegal, Tanzania, Ghana, and Zambia.
Requirements: Participants should have good communication skills and a strong desire to establish contact with people of another culture.
Age: Minimum 18 for Africa; 15 for the Caribbean.
Living Arrangements: Living is simple, with basic amenities.
Finances: The participation fee is $3,500.
Deadline: February 15.

Overseas Development Network

333 Valencia Street, Suite 330
San Francisco, CA 94103
Phone: (415) 431-4480

Organization: ODN is an international student-based organization committed to education about global poverty, hunger, and injustice. Believing that education and action are inseparable, ODN promotes responsible involvement of its members in addressing the problems and potential solutions of global development. ODN connects students with community-based development projects around the world and creates a dynamic network of people striving for global grassroots development.

Program: Among its longer term activities, ODN sponsors a unique summer volunteer opportunity called Bike-Aid, an annual cross-country bicycle trek which involves individuals in addressing global problems of poverty and injustice. Bike-Aid is the primary funding source for ODN-partnered grassroots development initiatives as well as for ODN's own development education programs. Each year, six groups of 20 riders set off from Seattle, Portland, San Francisco, and Los Angeles in mid-June; from Austin in mid-July; and from Montreal in early August. All groups converge on Washington, D.C. at the end of the summer.
Requirements: Participants should be self-motivated, interested in development issues, and ready for adventure. No previous cycling or fundraising experience is required.
Living Arrangements: Group accommodations vary along the way from campgrounds to churches to private homes.
Finances: Participants pay a registration fee of $150. Most accommodations and some meals are provided by hosts along each route. Other personal costs are the individual's responsibility and may vary, according to equipment, repair, food, and entertainment needs, from $300 to $1,000. Limited scholarship funds may be available.
Deadline: April 30. Enclose $5 (checks payable to Bike-Aid) for application and information packet.
Contact: Bike-Aid, Overseas Development Network.

Partners of the Americas

1424 K Street NW, Suite 700
Washington, DC 20005
Phone: (202) 628-3300

Organization: Partners is an inter-American volunteer technical assistance and cultural exchange organization which links 45 states with 31 countries in Latin America and the Caribbean.
Program: Volunteer specialists work as consultants traveling to the "partner" country to help with projects involving health care, agriculture, small business, community education, arts, and sports. Volunteers are expected to produce a trip report and continue their work in the partnership upon returning. Some sample partnership projects: the North Carolina-Bolivia partnership completed an early childhood stimulation workshop at an orphanage in Cochabamba; the Dominican-Dutchess County, New York partnership succeeded in building a solar-powered drying kiln to help develop that country's lumber industry; and the Long Island-St. Vincent partnership produced workshops that helped 227 women on that Caribbean island learn how to select and prepare nutritious foods for their families.
Requirements: Volunteers must have solid professional expertise in their field and the ability to communicate with their counterparts in another culture.
Living Arrangements: Volunteers usually stay with families or in modest hotels.
Persons with Disabilities: Partners actively seeks and encourages those with disabilities to fully participate in Partner projects and programs.
Finances: The volunteers' travel and accommodations during the service are provided. Out-of-pocket expenses usually total $50–$200. Specialists are asked to develop financial or material support for the project once they've returned home.
Deadline: None.
Contact: Applications should be made to local Partners committees. Contact the address above for a listing of Partnership presidents throughout the country.

Partnership for Service Learning

815 Second Avenue
Suite 315
New York, NY 10017
Phone: (212) 986-0989

Organization: The Partnership is a consortium of colleges, universities, and service agencies organized nationally and internationally, which provides opportunities for students to combine their formal studies with an international/intercultural experience through community service.
Program: Semester, year, summer, and January intersession programs are available in Ecuador, England and Scotland, France, India, Jamaica, Liberia, Mexico, the Philippines, and South Dakota. The programs combine academic study with community service. The studies are given through accredited colleges in the host

country; academic credit is granted from the student's home college. Service opportunities vary, but generally involve human services, teaching, health care, special education, English as a second language, and community development. The service takes place 20 to 35 hours a week. Undergraduates, recent graduates, professionals, and high school seniors are invited to apply.
Requirements: "Motivation to be of meaningful service is more important than special skills."
Age: Minimum 18.
Living Arrangements: Student participants usually live with families, at the host college, or in the service agency.
Finances: A fee which covers orientation, instruction, room, board, and related costs is charged. Participants make their own arrangements for transportation to and from workcamps and spending money. Financial aid can apply for registered students. Program costs range from $1,400 to $3,400.
Deadline: Two months before the start of the program.
Contact: Howard A. Berry, Linda A. Chisolm, Co-Directors.

"I found that I couldn't change the world, but I did teach four children to read."

Plenty International

P.O. Box 2306
Davis, CA 95617
Phone: (916) 753-0731

Organization: Plenty is an international development, educational, and environmental organization. It offers opportunities to committed volunteers who are willing to pay their own expenses to take part in projects in the U.S. and overseas.
Program: Volunteers mostly serve for one to three months. Examples of possible opportunities are: in Belize, providing technical support for soy foods utilization training; in Dominica, helping Carib Indians develop small business ventures and community services; in India, teaching soybean processing methods to rural and urban populations; and in the U.S., providing agricultural training for Native Americans.
Requirements: Vary according to the project.
Living Arrangements: Vary according to location.
Persons with Disabilities: Persons with disabilities are welcome.
Finances: Volunteers pay their own expenses and sometimes contribute to project budgets.
Deadline: None.
Contact: Peter Schweitzer, Executive Director.

Project Concern International/Options Service

P.O. Box 85323
San Diego, CA 92186.
Phone: (619) 279-9690

Organization: This is a nonprofit personnel agency which places health care and development specialists in rural areas of Africa, Asia, Eastern Europe, and North and South America. The agency's parent foundation is Project Concern.

Program: Volunteers may serve from two weeks to three months. They are all medical and health professionals who choose the positions that interest them from a regularly compiled list of openings. Some of the positions are more like jobs than voluntary service, but others fit into the latter category. Some examples of recent openings: a surgeon in Kenya to be in charge of a 120-bed hospital, registered nurses in Uganda to teach in a hospital, a doctor or nurse with childcare experience to work in an orphanage in rural India, ophthalmologists to do cataract surgery in primitive conditions in Nepal, etc.

Requirements: All applicants must be licensed in their field.

Age: Minimum 18.

Living Arrangements: Vary with assignment. Room and board are almost always provided; some positions also have salaries, stipends, travel funds, etc. Options charges a $10 annual fee for its services.

Persons with Disabilities: Options refers individuals to facilities; thus, the policy depends on the facility. Options will, however, refer anyone qualified for any position, regardless of their disability status.

Finances: Some positions include a stipend, travel allowance, and room and board; some, a travel allowance and room and board; others, only room and board.

Deadline: None.

Contact: Placement Director, Options Department.

Project ORBIS

330 West 42nd Street
Suite 1900
New York, NY 10036
Phone: (212) 244-2525

Organization: Project ORBIS is an international humanitarian organization that has been in operation since 1982. The objective of the project, the world's only flying teaching facility for ophthalmologists, nurses, and other eye care professionals, is to combat world blindness through education and to promote peaceful cooperation among nations.

Program: The ORBIS DC-8 aircraft, which houses an ultra-modern operating and examination room, spends 90 percent of its time in developing countries where the need for continuing ophthalmic education is most urgent. For one week, volunteer ophthalmologists (the visiting surgeons) join the DC-8 jet with its permanent international crew of 25 doctors, nurses, technicians, and administrators in order to demonstrate surgical skills to host country doctors. Through the use of a two-way

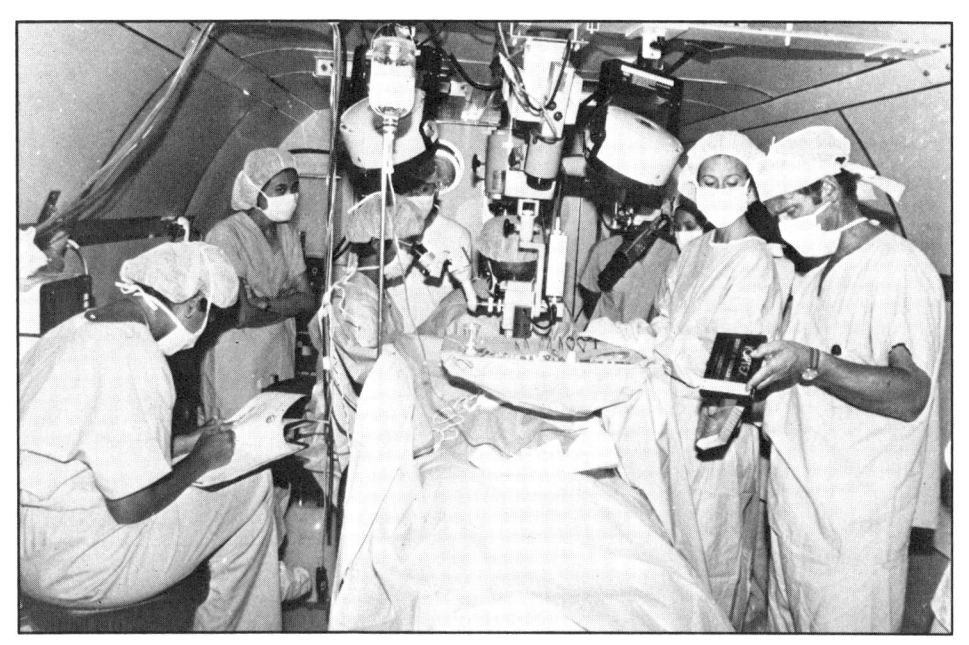

Project ORBIS volunteers at work in the on-board operating room.

audio/visual system, the host doctors are able to view and participate in the operational procedures performed by the visiting surgeons.
Requirements: Visiting surgeons must be in practice for at least two years post-residency and one year post-fellowship.
Living Arrangements: Volunteer surgeons stay in hotels with permanent members of the crew.
Persons with Disabilities: ORBIS does not discriminate.
Finances: ORBIS's funds are limited. Most visiting surgeons donate their time, expenses, and airfare (though hotel rooms are donated by the host country). ORBIS realizes that this can be an enormous burden on full-time academic professors and will do their best to help where they can.
Deadline: None.

Contact: Risa Kory, Director of Medical Coordination.

"ORBIS gets you back into a team spirit, which you can lose in your regular practice. You establish sincere relationships based on mutual respect and understanding."

Queen Elizabeth's Foundation for the Disabled

Lulworth Court
25 Chalkwell Esplanade
Westcliff-on-Sea
Essex SSO 8JQ
England

Organization: This organization operates a holiday home in Westcliff-on-Sea for physically disabled men and women aged 16 years and older.

Program: Volunteers work for one or two weeks at Lulworth Court, supplementing the permanent staff and insuring that the needs of the guests are met "with a minimum of fuss." "There is a cheerful and informal atmosphere at Lulworth Court, as we want our guests to enjoy doing everything we can offer and, as far as possible, to forget their disabilities."
Requirements: No experience is necessary—"simply common sense, adaptability, willingness to do whatever is required, a sense of humor, and reasonable physical strength."
Age: Minimum 18.
Living Arrangements: Volunteers live in an annex building in single or double rooms, sharing bath and toilet facilities.
Persons with Disabilities: It is not possible to accommodate persons with disabilities.
Finances: Room and board, plus a weekly stipend of £15, are provided.
Deadline: None.
Contact: Holiday Organizer.

R.E.M.P. ART.

1, rue des Guillemites
75004 Paris
Framce
Phone: (33-1) 42.71.96.55

Organization: R.E.M.P. ART. stands for the Union des Associations Animatrices de Chantiers de Sauvegarde pour la Rehabilitation et l'Entretien des Monuments et du Patrimoine Artistique.
Program: R.E.M.P. ART. workcamps involve the restoration of old buildings and monuments all over France. They last from a weekend to one month or longer.
Age: Minimum 18, although some 16- and 17-year-olds are considered.
Finances: An application fee of approximately $25 is charged, and there's a daily charge for room and board (approximately $5 to $8 per day).

Royal Society for Mentally Handicapped Children and Adults

119 Drake Street
Rochdale, Lancashire OL16 1PZ, England
Phone: (44-706) 54111

Organization: MENCAP is the largest organization in England providing services for mentally handicapped people and their families.
Program: Each summer MENCAP organizes holidays all over England for people of all ages with mental handicaps. The holidays may be held in schools, adventure centers, holiday houses, and guest houses, and are all staffed by volunteers who work from 9 to 16 days, about 12 to 14 hours per day. There are three kinds of holidays—one called "special care" where the ratio is one volunteer to one handicapped child or adult, another called "adventure holidays" where it's more likely for a volunteer to care for two people, and "guest house holidays," which are for mentally handicapped people over 18 who require less physical attention but more emotional support. Volunteers take

care of the personal needs of the people on holiday and share in the cooking, cleaning, laundry, etc.
Requirements: Volunteers need no special skills. "You need to be persevering with a mature and responsible attitude toward this demanding work. Expect to work hard and long hours."
Age: Minimum 18. Most are 18 to 25.
Living Arrangements: Volunteers live in holiday center dormitories.
Finances: Room and board are provided. Traveling expenses up to £20 are paid.
Deadline: None.

Service Archéologique du Musée de Douai

191, rue St. Albin
59500 Douai, France
Phone: (33-27) 87.26.63, ext.355

Organization: The aim of the organization is archaeological research.
Program: Volunteers work in Douai during the summer for a minimum of 15 days (recommended). The program runs from July 1 through August 31.
Requirements: No special skills are required. A knowledge of French is extremely helpful, but English is also acceptable.
Age: Minimum 18; 16 for French citizens.
Finances: Room and board are provided.
Deadline: June 20.
Contact: Pierre Demolon, Director of Archaeological Service.

Service Civil International—International Voluntary Service

Route 2, Box 506
Crozet, VA 22932
Phone: (804) 823-1826

Organization: SCI/IVS was founded in 1920 and is one of the older members of the voluntary workcamp movement.
Program: European countries have the most active branches, with summer workcamps from two to three weeks in length. SCI/IVS also has an exchange with Eastern European countries in the summer. SCI/IVS has organized workcamps in the U.S. since 1956. Workcamp projects have a range of sponsors: urban and rural community centers, peace centers, private institutions, Native American groups, etc. "The basic philosophy of SCI/IVS is 'Deeds not words.'" SCI/IVS promotes international understanding through practical service. SCI/IVS takes no political stands, but seeks to foster reconciliation of opposing groups, e.g., in Northern Ireland, children from Catholic and Protestant backgrounds.
Requirements: Volunteers must be willing to work from six to eight hours a day, sometimes in primitive conditions, sharing community chores. The language of the country is sometimes required.
Age: Minimum 16 for U.S. workcamps; 18 for workcamps abroad.
Living Arrangements: Volunteers live simply, sometimes in tents, sometimes in dormitories or one large

room. A sleeping bag is recommended equipment, and meals are prepared cooperatively.

Persons with Disabilities: Persons with mental or physical disabilities are encouraged to participate in SCI/IVS workcamps and are accepted on an individual basis.

Finances: There is an application fee of $75 for workcamps abroad, $35 for workcamps in the U.S. Room and board and health and accident insurance are provided. Volunteers must pay their own travel and incidental expenses.

Deadline: None.

Contact: SCI/IVS National Coordinator. An international workcamp list is available each April for $3.

Sioux Indian YMCAs

Box 218
Dupree, SD 57623
Phone: (605) 365-5232

Organization: This is a federation of 28 "nonbuilding" YMCAs in small, isolated Sioux reservation communities that serve area families.

Program: Volunteers serve for 9 to 10 weeks from March to May or June to August as community development aides, recreation leaders, counselors, cooks, teachers, etc. Every year there are four to six volunteers from other countries. Volunteers must attend a four- to five-day orientation program in Dupree which covers Sioux culture and reservation life and provides specifics about their placements.

Requirements: Experience is necessary for recreation work, counseling, camp skills, or working with children.

Age: Minimum 18.

Living Arrangements: Community development aides and recreation leaders usually live with families in small reservation communities; camp staff live in tepees.

Persons with Disabilities: As the camp is primitive, the organization believes it is inappropriate for persons with disabilities.

Finances: Room and board are provided; volunteers make their own travel arrangements.

Deadline: February 1 for spring programs; March 15 for summer.

Contact: Myrl Weaver, Executive Director.

SIW Internationale Vrijwilligerprojekten

Willemstraat 7
NL-3511 RJ Utrecht
Netherlands

Organization: This Dutch workcamp organization believes "that social problems have their causes in the structure of society and that solving these problems implies social changes. That is why SIW workcamps are directed towards awareness, commitment, and political action."

Program: SIW organizes about 10 international workcamps in the Netherlands each year. These usually consist of 20 young people from Europe and around the world. Each camp has a certain theme, to which the work project is directly related whenever possible. Past themes have been environmental protection, refugees, women's solidarity, and peace. Most

workcamps last three weeks during July and August.
Requirements: None.
Age: 18–30.
Living Arrangements: Lodging is "sufficient, though sometimes primitive"—in schools, community centers, farms, or tents, depending on the workcamp site.
Persons with Disabilities: Depending on the workcamp, certain disablities can be accommodated.
Finances: Volunteers pay a placement fee to the national workcamp organization in their own country. Room and board are provided, but travel to and from the workcamp site is the volunteer's responsibility.
Deadline: April 15.
Contact: Volunteers must apply through a national workcamp organization in their own country. For further information, U.S. volunteers should contact either the Council on International Educational Exchange or Volunteers for Peace (see these organizations' listings in this section).

Student Conservation Association

P.O. Box 550
Charlestown, NH 03603
Phone: (603) 826-4301

Organization: The Student Conservation Association offers volunteer opportunities for high school and college students to work on conservation projects throughout the U.S.
Program: Volunteers may work with endangered species, trail maintenance and construction, interpretation, etc. There are two types of service. The Resource Assistant (RA) Program runs for 12 weeks year round and is for those over 18. The High School Program runs for four to five weeks during the summer. Volunteers work for federal and state agencies like the National Park Service or the U.S. Fish and Wildlife Service in the continental U.S. as well as Hawaii, the U.S. Virgin Islands, Canada, Mexico, and Russia
Requirements: Some RA positions require specific academic training.
Age: Minimum 16 for the High School Program; 18 for the Resource Assistant Program.

Student Conservation Volunteers in Maine, with Mount Katahdin in the background.

Living Arrangements: Resource Assistants are provided housing. High School participants are provided camping equipment and food.
Persons with Disabilities: Persons with disabilities are accepted into the program depending on the organization's ability to place them in a position which can use their skills and provide facilities for them.
Finances: Resource Assistants are provided with a stipend for travel and food.
Deadline: March 1 for the High School Program; deadline varies for the Resource Assistant Program.
Contact: Recruitment Director.

"My experiences with SCA were definitely what formed, and then solidified, my interest in a conservation career."

Tallahatchie Development League

223 Front Street
P.O. Box 267
Tutwiler, MS 38963
Phone: (601) 345-8574

Organization: The League promotes community development in the areas of economics, education, and family life. It organizes people to deal with their problems and serves as a liaison between people and resources.
Program: Volunteers may participate in short-term or long-term projects that involve construction, teaching, Bible study, office work, or nutrition. Most volunteers come in preformed groups. Some projects that the League sponsors include meals on wheels, youth recreation, housing development programs, and a legal counseling program for people who need help in the area of domestic relations.
Requirements: Skills must match the placement.
Age: Minimum age is 14 for groups as long as there's an adult adviser.
Living Arrangements: Groups stay in individual rooms in private homes.
Persons with Disabilities: The League does not discriminate on any basis. Persons with disabilities are encouraged to apply.
Finances: Groups pay for their own food and some supplies.
Deadline: None.
Contact: Larry Haynes, Executive Director.

UNAREC

33 rue Campagne Premier
75014 Paris
France

Organization: UNAREC organizes workcamps all over France for volunteers from abroad and places French volunteers in workcamps in other countries.
Program: Volunteers may work restoring old houses and public buildings, creating new buildings and playgrounds, reestablishing old footpaths, maintaining river banks, protecting sand dunes, promoting alternative energy, and training unemployed youth. Assignments last about three weeks. Some examples: in Verneuil-en-Bourbonnais, the restoration of an old chapel designated to become a conference center and concert hall; the creation of a footpath on an island 15 kilometers from the

coast of Morbihan; the construction of a path with stairs leading to the chateau which looks over the city of Sommieres. Volunteers come from 25 different countries.
Requirements: "Motivation for manual work and collective life." Knowledge of French is required.
Age: Minimum 18.
Finances: Volunteers pay a placement fee to the national workcamp organization in their own country. Room and board are provided, but the cost of travel to and from the workcamp is the volunteer's responsibility.
Deadline: April 15.
Contact: Volunteers must apply through a national workcamp organization in their own country. For further information, U.S. volunteers must contact the Council on International Educational Exchange (see the organization's listing in this section).

United Nations Association International Youth Service

Temple of Peace
Cathays Park
Cardiff CF1 3AP
Wales

Organization: UNA organizes international workcamps as well as community day camp programs for local children.
Program: Volunteers are involved with playschemes for underprivileged children, activities for handicapped children and adults, and conservation workcamps. Projects are held from Easter to the end of summer and usually last two or three weeks. Each project accommodates between 5 and 15 volunteers.
Age: Minimum 18.
Persons with Disabilities: Volunteers with disabilities are accepted by arrangement.
Finances: Volunteers pay a placement fee to the national workcamp organization in their own country. Room and board are provided, but travel to and from the workcamp site is the volunteer's responsibility.
Deadline: April 15.
Contact: Volunteers must apply through a national workcamp organization in their own country. For further information, U.S. volunteers should contact either the Council on International Educational Exchange or Volunteers for Peace (see these organizations' listings in this section).

United States Forest Service—Alaska Region

P.O. Box 21628
Juneau, AK 99802-1628
Phone: (907) 586-8801

Organization: The Alaska Region of the U.S. Forest Service is responsible for the nation's two largest National Forests: the Tongass National Forest (17 million acres) in southeastern Alaska and the Chugach National Forest (6 million acres) in southern Alaska.
Program: Volunteer positions available in the Alaska Region include, but are not limited to: interpreters, archaeology aides, fishery aides,

wildlife habitat maintenance and protection aides, forestry aides, trail maintenance assistants, wilderness rangers, campground hosts, cooks, survey crew members, maintenance workers, clerical assistants, warehouse assistants, and information aides. Both short- and long-term opportunities are available. Volunteers may work full- or part-time.
Requirements: None, but those with skills are more easily placed.
Age: Minimum 16.
Living Arrangements: Accommodations vary from crew quarters at field locations to in-town apartments.
Persons with Disabilities: Persons with disabilities are welcomed.
Finances: Volunteers generally receive housing and a daily allowance of $23 for food. In some cases, housing is not provided.
Deadline: None.
Contact: Regional Volunteer Coordinator.

United States Forest Service—Northern Region

Federal Building
P.O. Box 7669
Missoula, MT 59807

Organization: The Northern Region of the U.S. Forest Service is responsible for federal lands in Montana, northern Idaho, western North Dakota, and part of northwest South Dakota.
Program: Volunteers are needed to work on conservation projects, campground hosting, wildlife management, and assisting with teaching and counseling in job corps centers. Opportunities can last from one day to years but are mainly available from May to October.
Requirements: None.
Age: No age limits; those under 16 require parental approval.
Living Arrangements: Some projects provide food and house volunteers in bunk houses, rental units, or tents.
Persons with Disabilities: Depending on the task, persons with disabilities are welcome to apply.
Finances: Room and board are sometimes provided.
Deadline: Open year round; for spring/summer openings, applications are needed by April.
Contact: Human Resource Programs.

United States Forest Service—Pacific Northwest Region

P.O. Box 3623
Portland, OR 97208
Phone: (503) 326-3816

Organization: The Pacific Northwest Region of the U.S. Forest Service maintains 19 national forests in Oregon and Washington.
Program: Volunteers are needed to maintain trails, campgrounds, wildlife, and timber.
Requirements: The organization tries to tailor jobs to match volunteers' skills.
Living Arrangements: Vary, but may be a bunkhouse or cabin.
Persons with Disabilities: The organization works to find ways to accommodate individual needs.

Finances: Full-time volunteers usually receive room and board; living allowances can be negotiated.
Deadline: None.
Contact: Volunteer Coordinator.

Vereinigung Junger Freiwilliger

Unter den Linden 36
1086 Berlin
Germany

Organization: VJF is a new, independent, student organization in Berlin offering workcamp projects in eastern Germany.
Program: Workcamps take place during the summer and last approximately two weeks. Projects often have an educational emphasis, providing discussion on topics of German history and current events while volunteers perform such tasks as renovating historic places or working on agricultural cooperatives.
Requirements: No special skills are required, though a knowledge of German is useful on some projects.
Age: Minimum 18.
Living Arrangements: Accommodations vary according to the project but are usually basic.
Finances: Volunteers pay a placement fee to the national workcamp organization in their own country. Room and board are provided, but the cost of travel to and from the workcamp is the volunteer's responsibility.
Deadline: April 15.
Contact: Volunteers must apply through a national workcamp association in their own country. For further information, U.S. volunteers should contact the Council on International Educational Exchange or Volunteers for Peace (see these organizations' listings in this section).

Voluntarios Internacionales México

Alfredo Elizondo 69
Col. Damian Carmona
C.P. 15450 México, D.F.
México

Organization: VIMEX organizes international workcamps in Mexico.
Program: Projects take place during the summer months. Volunteers work in groups of 14 on such projects as protection of endangered marine turtles and beach beautification.
Requirements: Volunteers should have a basic knowledge of Spanish.
Age: 18–30.
Living Conditions: Volunteers live in very basic accommodations, such as grass huts on the beach.
Finances: Volunteers pay a placement fee to the national workcamp organization in their own country. In addition, VIMEX charges an additional US$250, which covers everything after the volunteer's arrival in Mexico City: room and board, transportation to the workcamp, weekend trips. Volunteers are responsible for arranging their own transportation to Mexico City.
Deadline: April 15.
Contact: Volunteers must apply

through a national workcamp association in their own country. For further information, U.S. volunteers should contact the Council on International Educational Exchange, (see the organization's listing in this section).

Voluntary Service Slovenia

Askerceva 9
61000 Ljubljana
Slovenia

Organization: VSS organizes international workcamps in Slovenia.
Program: Summer volunteers are engaged in construction, renovation, ecological research, social work, peace work, and study workcamps in Slovenia.
Requirements: None.
Age: Minimum 18.
Living Arrangements: Accommodations are usually basic.
Finances: Volunteers pay a placement fee to the national workcamp organization in their own country. Room and board are provided, but the cost of travel to and from the workcamp is the volunteer's responsibility.
Deadline: April 15.
Contact: Volunteers must apply through a national workcamp association in their own country. For further information, U.S. volunteers should contact the Council on International Educational Exchange, Service Civil International—USA, or Volunteers for Peace (see these organizations' listings in this section).

Volunteer Optometric Service to Humanity

505 South Clay
Taylorville, IL 62568
Phone: (217) 824-6152

Organization: Founded in 1972, VOSH works to bring visual care to needy people throughout the world with emphasis on Third World countries. Although VOSH is vision-oriented, other doctors, surgeons, and dentists have traveled with VOSH teams.
Program: A typical VOSH mission includes five or more optometrists who examine eyes, two or more opticians to dispense glasses, and several optometric assistants. It is not unusual for such a team to examine 2,500 patients in one week. "The hours are long and the pace is hectic...the clinic may be in a village town hall or on a makeshift table in the middle of a rain forest." Volunteers serve for one week to one month, usually between September and June. Opportunities are in Africa, Asia, and the Americas.
Requirements: Ophthalmologists, optometrists, and lay people are needed.
Age: Minimum 18.
Living Arrangements: Facilities range from primitive to comfortable.
Finances: Sometimes room and board are provided, but more often volunteers pay for their own meals and lodging. Volunteers pay their own travel expenses and insurance.
Deadline: None.
Contact: James Hess, 5200 Douglas Drive, Crystal, MN 55429; (612) 537-3213.

Voluntary Workcamps Association of Ghana

P.O. Box 1540
Accra, Ghana

Organization: VOLU organizes workcamps in Ghana. It is dedicated to rural assistance as well as development.
Program: Volunteers work in small villages and towns on projects that involve unskilled manual labor such as digging, clearing brush, and mixing and pouring concrete in order to build roads, schools, street drains, or latrines.
Requirements: No special skills are required.
Age: Minimum 18.
Living Arrangements: Living conditions are basic: meals are cooked over open fires, there is no electricity, and sleeping is on the floor.
Persons with Disabilities: Disabled persons should write in advance to find out if a particular project features accessible worksites
Finances: Volunteers pay a fee to the national workcamp organization in their own country. Room and board are provided, but the cost of travel to and from the workcamp is the volunteer's responsibility.
Deadline: April 1.
Contact: Volunteers must apply through a national workcamp organization in their own country. U.S. volunteers should contact the Council on International Educational Exchange (see the organization's listing in this section).

Voluntary Workcamps Association of Nigeria

107 Herbert MacCaulay Street
Ebute Metta, Lagos
Nigeria

Organization: The association is nongovernmental, nonreligious, and nonpolitical. Its aim is to foster mutual intertribal and international relationships and peace through workcamps and other activities.
Program: Workcamps last from four weeks to six months, from July to September, and involve construction, social services, and self-help community development projects. Long-term development projects are also possible.
Requirements: Volunteers must be willing to serve. Skilled and professional volunteers are welcome.
Age: Minimum 18.
Living Arrangements: Volunteers live in hostels or with local families.
Finances: Volunteers pay a placement fee to the national workcamp organization in their own country. Room and board are provided, but the cost of travel to and from the workcamp is the volunteer's responsibility.
Deadline: May.
Contact: Volunteers must apply through a national workcamp organization in their own country. For further information, U.S. volunteers should contact Volunteers for Peace or Service Civil International—International Voluntary Service (see these organizations' listings in this section).

Volunteers for Peace

43 Tiffany Road
Belmont, VT 05730
Phone: (802) 259-2759

Organization: Formed in 1981 for the purpose of "promoting peaceful relations among nations," VFP is a non-profit corporation which recruits Americans and Canadians for workcamps abroad and American and foreign volunteers for domestic workcamps. It also provides information to potential host communities in the U.S.
Program: Volunteers perform varied services in 36 countries and the U.S. The foreign workcamps are mainly in Central America, Europe, North and West Africa, Turkey, and republics of the former Soviet Union. Participants join volunteers from at least three other countries in social, environmental, conservation, restoration, archeological, or agricultural work. The length of service is usually two to three weeks, May through September. Multiple placements are common.
Requirements: None.
Age: Minimum 18, although there are limited opportunities for ages 15 to 18.
Living Arrangements: Accommodations vary with the worksite; volunteers may stay in dormitories, tents, churches, private homes, schools, etc.
Persons with Disabilities: Some workcamps are designed specifically for persons with disabilities. Those who think they can complete the work are accepted.
Finances: Volunteers must raise their own funds and arrange and pay for all transportation costs. On average a $100 registration fee is required per workcamp for foreign placements.

Bulgarian volunteer gives American friend a lift at Volunteers for Peace Workcamp in the state of Maryland.

Meals, accommodations, and accident insurance are provided.
Deadline: No deadline, but most volunteers register in April and May.
Contact: Peter Coldwell, Executive Director.

Winant-Clayton Volunteers

109 East 50th Street
New York, NY 10022
Phone: (212) 751-1616, ext. 271

Organization: WCV is a nonprofit organization which arranges U.S.-U.K. volunteer exchanges. While nondenominational, WCV has a traditional association with the Church of England and the Episcopal Church.
Program: Each summer for eight weeks, groups of English citizens come to work in the northeastern U.S., while groups of U.S. citizens work in London and other British cities. Volunteers work in youth clubs, homeless shelters, facilities for the physically and mentally disabled, playschools for disadvantaged children, etc. Participants have two or three weeks of free vacation time abroad following their assignment.
Requirements: None.
Age: Minimum 18.
Living Arrangements: Facilities vary widely.
Persons with Disabilities: Each case is considered individually; disabled volunteers have served in the past.
Finances: WCV charges a $15 application fee. Participants pay for their own transportation to and from Great Britain. Once there, volunteers receive room, board, and $15 per week.
Deadline: January 31.
Contact: Virginia Peters.

Workcamps Office of DEMISZ

Könyves Kálmán krt. 76
1087 Budapest VIII
Hungary

Organization: DEMISZ is the Hungarian Democratic Youth Federation.
Program: The Workcamps Office organizes workcamps in Hungary during the summer months. Most projects involve nature conservation or parklands preservation, placing volunteers in very beautiful natural settings.
Requirements: No special skills are required, though a knowledge of German is useful on some projects.
Age: Minimum 18.
Living Arrangements: Accommodations vary from lodgings in youth hostels to rustic wooden cottages with thatched rooves.
Finances: Volunteers pay a placement fee to the national workcamp organization in their own country. Room and board are provided, but the cost of travel to and from the workcamp is the volunteer's responsibility.
Deadline: April 15.
Contact: Volunteers must apply through a national workcamp association in their own country. For further information, U.S. volunteers should contact the Council on International Educational Exchange (see the organization's listing in this section).

YMCA International Camp Counselor Program

356 West 34th Street, Third Floor
New York, NY 10001
Phone: (212) 563-3441

Organization: ICCP promotes person-to-person contacts in youth camps around the world. "Working side by side with other local young men and women as counselors in a camp (or camp-like setting), you will have the chance to gain the kind of cultural understanding that few tourists can."

Program: ICCP participants work at camps in Africa, Asia, Australia, Europe, or Latin America for about one or two months in the summer. Young people from abroad also come to the U.S. to work in camps through ICCP. Positions vary—counselors may be asked to lead sports, music, dance, nature study, sailing, swimming, etc. ICCP sends applicants a list of openings so that they may choose the one most suitable.

Requirements: Applicants should have some experience working with groups of children. Specific skills needed vary with the camp. Some camps require second language fluency; others do not, although some knowledge of the language of the host country is highly recommended. ICCP participants must also be flexible, independent, resourceful, patient, and have a sense of humor.

Age: Varies with the assignment, but usually between 20 and 30 years.

Living Arrangements: Participants live with other counselors on the camp site.

Finances: There's a $150 application fee. Participants must pay their own transportation costs, but insurance and room and board are provided. Some camps may provide pocket money and domestic transportation to the camp.

Deadline: February 15.
Contact: Lisa Ortiz, Director.

Youth Service Opportunities Project

15 Rutherford Place
New York, NY 10003
Phone: (212) 598-0973

Organization: YSOP organizes weekend workcamps in the New York metropolitan area.

Program: Volunteers spend a weekend working in soup kitchens, family shelters, and drop-in centers, serving people who are homeless.

Requirements: None.

Living Arrangements: Simple accommodations are provided. Volunteers are asked to bring sleeping bags.

Persons with Disabilities: Disabled persons should call or write in advance to find out if a particular camp features accessible worksites.

Finances: A fee of $55 is charged. Meals are included.

Deadline: One week before the actual weekend. Call or write for schedule.

Contact: Beth Burns, Director.

"My ideas and feelings about the homeless were changed in a positive way by the workcamp. Most of the time we are afraid of the homeless and we forget they are human just like us. YSOP helped me to remember."

PART FOUR
Medium/Long-Term Placements

Alabama Council on Human Relations

P.O. Box 409
Auburn, AL 36830
Phone: (205) 821-8336

Organization: ACHR administers a variety of programs that assist low-income people such as Head Start, Community Services Block Grant, and the Alabama Coalition Against Hunger.
Program: Volunteers serve for one year doing child care work, community organizing, teaching, construction, or social work.
Requirements: These depend on the program; Head Start teachers must have a teaching degree, community organizers must be experienced.
Age: Minimum 20.
Living Arrangements: Volunteers make their own arrangements with help from the ACHR staff.
Persons with Disabilities: ACHR encourages those with disabilities to apply. Provisions have been made for access.
Finances: Volunteers must be entirely self-supporting.
Deadline: None.
Contact: Nancy S. Spears, Program Director.

Alderson Hospitality House

Greenbrier and High Streets
P.O. Box 579
Alderson, WV 24910
Phone: (304) 445-2980

Organization: The Hospitality House opened in 1977 to welcome visitors to the Federal Women's Prison in Alderson. The Hospitality House is "in the Catholic Worker tradition" and is not a part of the federal prison.
Program: Volunteers staff the Hospitality House. They must have an ability "to deal personally with a wide variety of people at any time, day or night." Maturity, flexibility, and willingness to live in Christian community are important.
Requirements: No special skills are required, Spanish is helpful.
Age: Minimum 20.
Living Arrangements: Volunteers have their own room in the Hospitality House.
People with Disabilities: The Hospitality House is open to accepting people with disabilities depending on the House's needs and the needs of the individual. The House sits on the side of a mountain and is not wheelchair accessible.
Finances: Room and board are provided.
Deadline: None.
Contact: John Parfitt, Co-Director.

American Refugee Committee

2344 Nicollet Avenue, Suite 350
Minneapolis, MN 55404
Phone: (612) 872-7060

Organization: Originally founded to assist in the resettlement of refugees in Minnesota and Illinois, ARC also provides health care services and training programs in their countries of origin, particularly Cambodia, Thailand, and Malawi.

Program: In addition to part-time opportunities in Chicago and Minneapolis, ARC needs medical personnel for one year of overseas service.
Requirements: Volunteers must be licensed professionals—medical doctors, registered nurses, midwives, engineers, psychiatrists, psychiatric nurses, and physicians' assistants. Personnel in Cambodia are required to learn Khmer. Volunteers must be in excellent health.
Living Arrangements: Volunteers live in individual bedrooms, sharing all other facilities in group housing.
Finances: Volunteers receive a stipend of $738 a month, which covers costs of food. Room is provided, as is insurance. Some salaried positions are available.
Deadline: None.
Contact: Marleah Jex, Associate, International Programs.

Année Diaconale

Service Protestant de la Jeunesse
rue du Champ de Mars, 5
B-1050 Bruxelles
Belgium

Organization: The organization is a youth service branch affiliated with the Protestant church in Belgium.
Program: Volunteers spend between 10 months and one year in Christian institutions in Belgium and other countries. Approximately 15 volunteers a year are placed in homes for children, young women, the elderly, and the handicapped.
Requirements: Volunteers should be fluent in French and have a Christian background.
Age: 18–25.
Finances: Volunteers receive room and board, traveling expenses, and a monthly stipend of FB 4,000.
Deadline: None.

Annunciation House

1003 East San Antonio
El Paso, TX 79901
Phone: (915) 545-4509

Organization: Annunciation House is a private organization founded 14 years ago, with the belief that "the Gospel calls us all to the poor." It operates several houses on either side of the U.S.-Mexico border, in the cities of El Paso and Juarez, offering hospitality to the homeless, particularly Central American refugees and the undocumented. Annunciation House comes out of a Catholic tradition and operates from a Christian faith perspective.
Program: Volunteers are needed to staff emergency and homeless shelters, to provide immigration/refugee services to Hispanics, to construct and maintain buildings, and to provide health care and social services. Volunteers are asked to commit a minimum of one year. Annunciation House also sponsors a 10-week Summer Internship Program (see under Short-Term Projects).
Requirements: A college degree and knowledge of Spanish are very helpful. It is important for volunteers to realize that they must be open to doing whatever needs to be done.
Age: Minimum 19.
Living Arrangements: Volunteers live in dormitory-style rooms.

Persons with Disabilities: Each applicant is considered individually.
Finances: Room, board, minor medical expenses, shampoo, soap, washing machines, and personal items are provided.
Deadline: Two weeks prior to one of the specific arrival dates for new volunteers: January 20, March 20, June 1, August 15, and November 1.
Contact: Ruben L. Garcia, Director, or Sr. Stella Dolan, Volunteer Coordinator.

"I am amazed by the inner strength and hope of our guests despite their difficult situations. The atmosphere of the house is one of happiness."

Association of Episcopal Colleges

815 Second Avenue
New York, NY 10017
Phone: (212) 986-0989

Association of Episcopal Colleges volunteers clearing a field for a children's playground in Appalachia.

Organization: This is a membership organization of colleges with past and present ties to the Episcopal Church.
Program: The Association places college students and recent graduates from any college in one of more than 30 locations in the U.S. and overseas to serve for periods from one month to one year. Volunteers teach children, the handicapped, or adults in literacy or job skills; work in health care facilities; assist in soup kitchens and homeless shelters; and organize community development projects. There are two types of volunteer opportunities. Service-Learning combines academic study (for college credit) with volunteer service and is available through cooperation with the Partnership for Service-Learning in Ecuador, England, France, India, Jamaica, Liberia, Mexico, the Philippines, and in South Dakota. Students Serving Others places students in a ministering agency sponsored or supported by the Episcopal or Anglican Church, to work and learn under the direction of a qualified professional care-giver.
Requirements: Evidence of commitment, maturity, and stability. Minimum foreign language required in some programs (Ecuador, France, Mexico).
Age: Minimum 18.
Living Arrangements: These vary with location—dorms, private

homes—and are arranged in advance by the Association.
Finances: Student's financial aid and loans should be applicable to the service-learning programs. Other programs' costs vary from small placement fee to those providing room, board, and small stipend to several providing salary. In all cases students pay transportation costs.
Persons with Disabilities: Participation is possible in some locations. Inquiries welcome.
Deadline: Varies with program, but generally two months prior to departure.

"I learned that I can't change the economy of Latin America, but I taught four children to read."

Boys Hope

4200 Ripa
St. Louis, MO 63125
Phone: (314) 544-1250

Organization: Boys Hope was founded in 1977 in Saint Louis, Missouri, to serve abused, abandoned, and neglected youths. The mission of Boys Hope is to provide a family-like home environment and Jesuit-influenced college preparatory education to capable and needy youths. The program is presently operative in 11 locations: Chicago; Cincinnati; Cleveland; Detroit; New Orleans; New York; Northeast Ohio; Orange County, California; Phoenix; Pittsburgh; and St. Louis. Boys join the program when they are between 10 and 14 and can remain with Boys Hope through high school.

Program: Volunteers are needed to act as houseparents, teachers, and social workers. They are asked to serve a minimum of one year.
Requirements: Houseparents must have a B.A., teachers must be certified, and social workers must have an M.A.
Age: Minimum 21.
Living Arrangements: Volunteers live in the group home; each has a private bedroom.
Finances: Room and board, insurance, and a $200 monthly stipend are provided.
Deadline: None.
Contact: John A. Ryan, National Program Director.

Brethren Volunteer Service

1451 Dundee Avenue
Elgin, IL 60120
Phone: (708) 742-5100

Organization: This is a Christian service program sponsored by the Church of the Brethren and cooperatively linked with the Disciples of Christ. BVS is dedicated to advocating justice, peacemaking, serving basic human needs, and maintaining the integrity of creation. It has over 200 positions available in 38 states in the U.S. and 18 nations abroad.
Program: Volunteers provide a variety of community services including education, health care, office work, construction work, and ministry to children, youth, senior citizens, homeless, victims of domestic violence, prisoners, refugees, persons with AIDS, and others. Positions in the U.S. require a one-year commit-

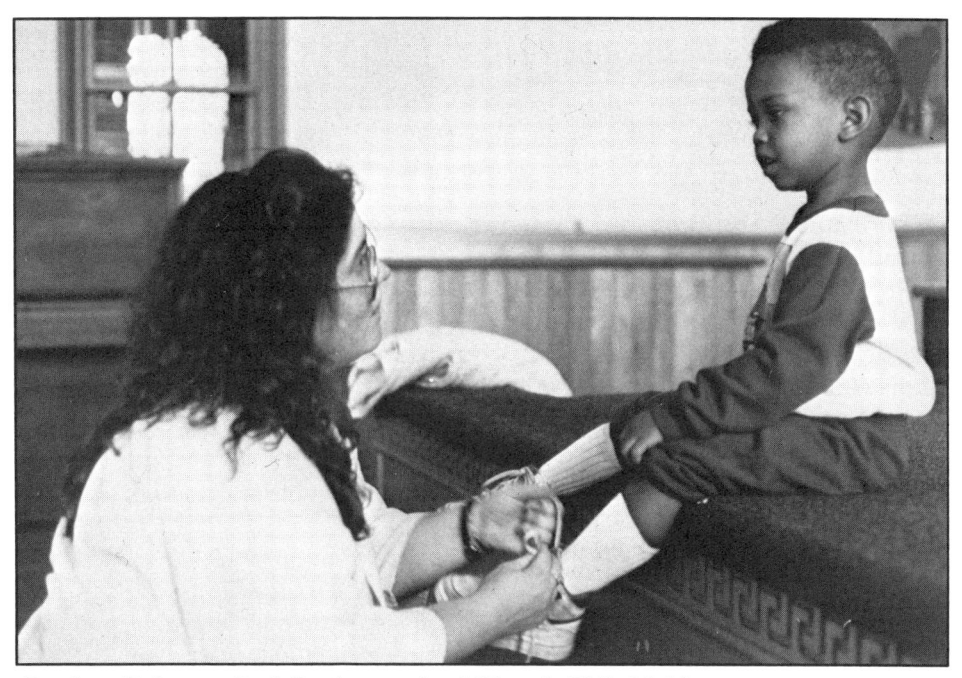

Brethren Volunteer Barb Davis cares for children in Philadelphia.

ment; overseas positions require two years. Service begins with a three-week orientation (offered four times a year) which examines a wide range of topics including peace and justice issues, hunger, stress management, Third World concerns, cross-cultural understanding, poverty, etc.

Requirements: Volunteers must be in good physical and mental health. They must be willing to "examine and study Christian faith" and must have completed high school or the equivalent. Requirements for special skills vary with projects. A college degree or equivalent life experience is required for overseas assignment.

Age: Minimum 18.

Living Arrangements: Volunteers may live independently, with other volunteers, or with families.

Persons with Disabilities: BVS has previously utilized persons with disabilities (blind, hearing-impaired, walking disabled). All applications are handled on a case by case basis.

Finances: Transportation costs to and from the project, room and board, a monthly stipend, and medical coverage are provided by the BVS.

Deadline: Six weeks before each orientation.

Contact: Debra Eisenbise, Recruitment.

"In BVS, 29 years of life experience and 18 years of formal education were sifted and sorted, distilled and purified, and funneled into my heart. BVS bridged that longest human distance in me or anyone, that distance between the head and the heart."

Brother Benno Foundation

Post Office Box 308
Oceanside, CA 92049
Phone: (619) 439-1244

Organization: The Brother Benno Foundation, established in 1983, operates a shelter and provides hot meals to the homeless community. The organization also provides job counseling, showers, clothing, and medical services.
Program: Volunteers help cook, wash dishes, distribute clothing, and maintain the shelter. An orientation period of one month is required. Volunteers serve for at least a year.
Requirements: No special skills are necessary.
Age: Minimum 21.
Living Arrangements: Volunteers live at the shelter.
Persons with Disabilities: No special accommodations are available.
Finances: Room and board and a small stipend are provided.
Deadline: None.
Contact: Patricia Leslie, Associate Director.

Camphill Village Trust

The Camphill School
Central Office
Bieldside
Aberdeen ABI 9EP, Scotland
Phone: (44-224) 867935

Organization: The Camphill Village Trust sponsors a number of volunteer projects, including Newton Dee Village, a community where mentally handicapped people work "to find security in a family setting and the satisfaction of purposeful work."
Program: Located about five miles west of Aberdeen, the Village is comprised of 185 people in 16 households. Volunteers serve for 6 to 12 months, but U.S. participants should serve at least a full year. Assignments vary, but volunteers may work in work shops, act as housemothers, or do farming.
Requirements: No degrees are required, but skills in cooking, sewing, and carpentry are helpful, and "an interest in spiritual matters" is necessary.
Age: Minimum 21.
Living Arrangements: Houses vary in size from 6 to 20 people, and each runs as an independent unit.
Finances: Room and board, insurance, and a small monthly stipend are provided. U.S. participants must pay their own travel expenses.
Deadline: None.

Caritas Mission

P.O. Box 129
Frenchville, PA 16836
Phone: (814) 263-4177

Organization: Caritas Mission is a Christian ministry which provides various services to the poor and disadvantaged of Clearfield County, Pennsylvania. "More than a nine to five job, it involves remaining open to the needs of hospitality and the demands of flexibility that arise in meeting the emergency needs of the people to whom we minister."
Program: Activities may include home repairs, providing transporta-

tion, visiting and/or caring for the sick and elderly, participating in meals-on-wheels, working in special programs for children such as recreation or tutoring, handling emergency housing problems, or assisting in retreat programs for adults and/or youth. Volunteers serve for six months to a year or longer.
Requirements: "Good health, a generous heart, flexibility and a willingness to learn."
Age: Minimum 19.
Living Arrangements: There are separate male and female dormitory facilities; all meals are eaten together. "We live a life of simplicity."
Persons with Disabilities: Applications from volunteers with disabilities are accepted depending on the disabilities. Because of the nature of the work, volunteers with mental or emotional disabilities are not accepted.
Finances: Room and board are provided. The long-term volunteer is asked to pay $135 for the first month's stay. After the first three months, volunteers receive a monthly stipend of $30 for personal expenses.
Deadline: None.
Contact: Director of Volunteers.

Casa Juan Diego

Houston Catholic Worker
P.O. Box 70113
Houston, TX 77270
Phone: (713) 864-4994 or 869-7376

Organization: Casa Juan Diego is a Catholic Worker House of Hospitality serving refugees from Central America and Spanish-speaking women and children who have been abused. It is also a major distributor of food and clothing to the poor of the city. "Catholic Worker lives are interwined with the works of mercy found in the Gospel of Matthew, Chapter 25. They try to take the Lord at His word who said, 'What you do to the least of my brethren you do to me.'" The work is hard but satisfying.
Program: Volunteers serve for one to two years, or more. They participate in every aspect of the operation of the Casa—transportation, cooking, cleaning, and working with guests.
Requirements: A college degree is preferred but not absolutely required. "An ability to work with people, to utilize supervision appropriately, and a knowledge of Spanish or a willingness to learn" are important. A personal telephone interview is required.
Age: Minimum 21.
Living Arrangements: Volunteers have their own rooms in the Casa.
Finances: Room and board and a small weekly stipend are provided.
Deadlines: May 1 and August 1.
Contact: Mark Zwick, Director.

"For me, working at Casa Juan Diego has been very valuable and enjoyable. I really believe that the Gospel of Jesus according to Matthew, Chapter 25, is being carried out here. The work is challenging and is given directly to the guests who live here and the surrounding community. Sharing faiths, resources and the work in community is truly a wonderful and exciting experience."

Casa Ricardo Chacon

P.O. Box 1041
Fort Worth, TX 76101
Phone: (817) 877-3705

Organization: Casa Ricardo Chacon is a nonprofit organization that provides temporary residency to Central Americans who have fled their countries for fear for their lives or liberty due to their religious or political beliefs, as well as providing cultural orientation, medical and dental care, and a variety of other types of assistance.
Program: Volunteers serve for a minimum of three to six months, providing such services as translation, cultural orientation, transportation of residents to appointments, teaching English, monitoring the house, and doing office work.
Requirements: Working Spanish is required.
Age: Minimum 21.
Living Arrangements: Volunteers have private rooms within the shelter.
Persons with Disabilities: Casa Ricardo Chacon has a nondiscriminatory policy. Persons with disabilities are provided with full bathroom facilities and a place to sleep on the first floor.
Finances: Volunteers receive room and board, $50 a month, and dental and health insurance.
Deadline: None.
Contact: Chris Daniels, Assistant Director.

Catholic Medical Mission Board

10 West 17th Street
New York, NY 10011-5765
Phone: (212) 242-7757

Organization: CMMB ships medicine to 6,000 missions in 60 Third World countries and recruits and processes volunteer medical personnel for service, without remuneration, to Third World missions for periods of one month to two or more years.
Program: Medical personnel are stationed in Africa, Asia, the Caribbean, Central and South America, India, and Oceania.
Requirements: A degree in medicine, dentistry, or technology. State licenses are required for R.N.s and P.N.s. Language requirements depend upon location.
Living Arrangements: Depending on the individual mission, accommodations are provided either on the mission compound or nearby.
Persons with Disabilities: CMMB accepts persons with disabilities if the disability permits service.
Finances: Volunteers receive room and board. Those who serve six months or more usually receive a modest stipend. Insurance is the responsibility of missions capable of providing such services.
Deadline: None.
Contact: Leo T. Tarpey, Placement Director.

Catholic Volunteers in Florida

P.O. Box 702
Goldenrod, FL 32733-0702
Phone: (407) 677-8005

Organization: The Catholic Volunteers in Florida (CVs) seek to promote the values of social justice through an experience of direct service and increased social awareness with people who do not have access to educational, cultural, social and/or economic resources. The CVs respond to needs identified by Catholic bishops, local parishes, Catholic and community social service agencies, and Catholic schools. The CVs incorporate an Augustinian heritage throughout the volunteer experience and each volunteer sets goals for personal and spiritual growth while in service.
Program: Volunteers serve for a period of one year (renewable) in Florida. Types of placement include business managers, child care workers, counselors, disabled group home workers, elementary teachers, house parents, nurses, religious education coordinators, shelter assistants, social workers, and volunteer coordinators.
Requirements: Volunteers must be U.S. citizens and Christian. Fluency in Spanish is helpful for some sites. Educational requirements are dependent upon the needs of the service site. Work experience is helpful; applicants should have previous part-time volunteer experience; should be flexible, positive, and self-motivated, with interest in social justice. Must be willing to participate in CV development program, which includes three weekend retreats and an eight-day formation program.
Age: Minimum 20.
Living Arrangements: Volunteers may live alone, in community with other volunteers, with local families, or in a religious community.
Finances: Room and board, medical and life insurance, and a monthly stipend of $100 are provided. The volunteer pays one-third of transportation costs to the initial interview in Florida.
Deadline: None.
Contact: Gina Cawley, Volunteer Coordinator.

"I had so much. I had two parents who were married and loved each other, and I had a nice home and no financial worries in college. I wanted to give something of myself back."

Cecil Houses

2/4 Priory Road
Kew, Richmond
Surrey TW9 3DG
England

Organization: This is a charity and housing association that operates residential care homes for the elderly, sheltered accommodation for the elderly, and hostels for women.
Program: Volunteers serve for four months to one year and are involved in caring for the elderly, domestic work, and assistance in the hostels for homeless women.
Requirements: No special skills are required.
Age: Minimum 18.

Living Arrangements: Volunteers are housed in shared simple accommodations.
Persons with Disabilities: Persons with moderate disabilities are encouraged to apply.
Finances: Volunteers receive room and board and a modest stipend.
Deadline: None.
Contact: Mrs. M. Richmond

Centro Adelante Campesino

P.O. Box 939
El Mirage, AZ 85335
Phone: (602) 583-9830

Organization: Centro is a nonprofit, volunteer based farm worker community organization and service center. It provides emergency food supplies, clothing, referral services, community outreach voices, and cultural activities to farm workers and other low-income or unemployed people and their families. It has a youth program and a home-based day care program.
Program: Volunteers may teach English or tutor other subjects, help conduct nutrition and gardening classes, work in our community garden and food bank, write proposals, or do typing and bookkeeping. If participants have other interests or strengths they should specify these. Centro is located in western Maricopa county, just west of Phoenix. The length of service is flexible. Volunteers must be willing to work at a variety of tasks. Typing skills are helpful. Some Spanish is desirable, but not necessary.
Age: Minimum 18.

Persons with Disabilities: The organization is "open to participation by anyone, including those with disabilities. We consider uniqueness of participants to be an asset."
Finances: Volunteers are responsible for their own expenses.
Deadline: None.
Contact: Alicia Rodriguez, Director, or Margaret Carl. (Send letter of introduction.)

Cheyenne River Youth Project

P.O. Box 1159
Eagle Butte, SD 57625
Phone: (605) 964-8200

Organization: The Cheyenne River Youth Project is a youth activities center on the Cheyenne River Sioux Reservation, providing tutoring, recreation, and arts activities.
Program: Volunteers are needed to work with Native American children and also to do program planning and fundraising.
Requirements: None, but experience working with Native Americans or children is preferred.
Age: Minimum 19.
Living Arrangements: Volunteers live in a two-bedroom apartment attached to center.
Finances: Volunteers receive $100 a month ($180 if they volunteer for 12 months or more). Room is provided and volunteers are eligible for a food assistance program.
Deadline: None.
Contact: Danette Albers, Project Coordinator.

Christian Appalachian Project

235 Lexington Street
Lancaster, KY 40444
Phone: (606) 792-2219

Organization: The Christian Appalachian Project is a Christian service organization founded to assist people in the Appalachian region of eastern Kentucky.
Program: Volunteer opportunities are available in programs ranging from child development centers to elderly visitation to residential programs. The volunteer program focuses on a life of prayer, family-style living, and service. Permanent volunteers serve for one year or longer; temporary volunteers serve for a minimum of three weeks. Summer opportunities are available.
Requirements: "We seek, first and foremost, a Christian purpose, positive attitude, ability to learn to relate to others, and flexibility."
Age: Minimum 21 for long-term volunteers; 18 for short-term volunteers.
Living Arrangements: Volunteers live together. Meals, morning and evening prayers, and household duties are shared.
Finances: Room and board, a monthly stipend, and health insurance are provided for long-term volunteers. Transportation is provided to and from the work site.
Deadline: None.
Contact: Kathy Kluesener.

Christian Foundation for Children and Aging

One Elmwood Avenue
Kansas City, KS 66103-3798
Phone: (913) 384-6500

Organization: The Christian Foundation for Children and Aging was founded by Catholic lay people in 1981. Its purpose is to mobilize support for missionaries working with the poor and needy in developing countries and to promote sharing and appreciation between peoples.
Program: Volunteers serve from six months to a lifetime, providing such services as child care, health care, construction, and teaching. Volunteers are placed in Mexico, Guatemala, Honduras, El Salvador, the Dominican Republic, Nicaragua, Costa Rica, Saint Kitts, Haiti, Colombia, Venezuela, Chile, Bolivia, Peru, Brazil, the Philippines, India, Kenya, and Madagascar.
Requirements: Volunteer experience is important. A high school education and for many positions a college education are necessary. Functional Spanish is required for Latin American placements.
Age: Minimum 21.
Living Arrangements: Volunteers live together with a religious community, with local families, or in a children's home.
Persons with Disabilities: All are invited to apply. Special provisions have been made for disabled volunteers. For example, a ramp was installed in a children's home in Yaritagua, Venezuela.
Finances: Volunteers are self-funded,

Christian Foundation volunteer Phil Cook with Cochi, an orphan, in San Andres Itzapa, Guatemala.

raising support before traveling to cover transportation, insurance, and personal expenses. Room and board are provided depending upon the location of placement.
Deadline: None.
Contact: Victoria Hoffman, Director of Volunteer Services.

Church World Service

National Council of the Churches of Christ in the USA
475 Riverside Drive, Room 668
New York, NY 10115
Phone: (212) 870-2368

Organization: This is the agency of the NCCC which provides help with emergencies in other countries, development assistance, and refugee services.
Program: Volunteers, almost always medical personnel, are needed when emergency programs are created, in response to extraordinary situations. At such times, volunteers serve for three months to a year. There is no ongoing program for volunteers.
Requirements: Medical personnel must have full certification.
Age: Beyond college age.
Living Arrangements: These vary according to assignment.
Finances: Room and board, a small stipend, and transportation expenses are provided.
Deadline: None.
Contact: Paul W. Yount, Jr., Director-Overseas Personnel.

City Volunteer Corps

838 Broadway, 3rd floor
New York, NY 10003
Phone: (212) 475-6444

Organization: The City Volunteer Corps is the nation's largest urban youth service program, enrolling New York City residents in a year of full-time or part-time community service work.
Program: Every year, over 600 City Volunteers provide New York City with over 300,000 hours of service on more than 300 projects with city agencies and nonprofit organizations. Projects, which take place throughout the city, include tutoring public school children, caring for the elderly, revitalizing parks, and converting vacant lots into safe play areas for children. City Volunteers, working in teams of 10 to 15 young

City Volunteer at work in a Chinatown daycare center.

people, complete several projects throughout the five boroughs. City Volunteers work seven hours a day, five days a week. In addition to providing service, volunteers attend classes to meet their individual academic needs. Classes offered include English as a Second Language, Adult Basic Education, GED, college preparatory and college-level classes. All prospective volunteers attend a seven-day residential training program in upstate New York where they participate in team-building activities and attend workshops focusing on developing communication and leadership skills.

Requirements: No special skills, training, or degrees are required to volunteer.
Age: 17–20.
Living Arrangements: Volunteers are responsible for their own living arrangements, except at training camp.
Finances: Volunteers receive a stipend of $100 per week and upon the successful completion of a year, are awarded a $5,000 scholarship or $2,500.
Deadline: None.

"I have grown within myself and have learned to accept individuals for who they are. I have learned the true meaning of a team, which is love, trust, and respect. It has been a privilege to serve a year in the City Volunteer Corps among new friends."

"When anyone asks, I tell them that CVC is a great thing to be part of. It's different from anything else I've ever done. There's really nothing else like it."

Club UNESCO "Martin Luther King"

5451 Liberte V
BP 10430 Dakar
Senegal

Organization: This UNESCO affiliate performs social services throughout Senegal.
Program: The Club UNESCO "Martin Luther King" began a literacy campaign in Senegal five years ago. Volunteers serve as teachers.
Requirements: Volunteers should have teaching experience, as well as knowledge of French or Wolof.
Age: Minimum 19.
Living Arrangements: Volunteers are responsible for their own living arrangements, though housing is inexpensive.
Finances: Participants receive a monthly salary of approximately $150.
Deadline: None.
Contact: Paco Garcia, Coordinator R.A.C.

Coalition for the Homeless

1234 Massachusetts Avenue NW
Washington, DC 20005
Phone: (202) 347-8870

Organization: This nonprofit agency operates two emergency, overnight shelters, three transitional homes, and 28 apartments for homeless families. The agency provides a range of social services to assist homeless Washingtonians in becoming self-sufficient.
Program: Volunteers are needed in all of the facilities. Volunteers serve food, counsel clients, and act as tutors.
Requirements: The ability to work independently and to get along with a diverse group of people is necessary. Patience and compassion are also needed.
Age: Minimum 17.
Living Arrangements: Volunteers make their own living arrangments.
Finances: Volunteers are self-supporting.
Deadline: None.
Contact: Diane Flanagan-Montgomery, Executive Director.

Community for Creative Non-Violence

425 2nd Street NW
Washington, DC 20001
Phone: (202) 393-1909

Organization: CCNV has been serving Washington's homeless for nearly two decades. All members serve as full-time volunteers, receiving only room and board. Volunteers live and work in the 1,400 bed shelter in the heart of the nation's capitol. "Our life together has a spiritual foundation, expressed in a variety of ways...we have come together to serve directly and through resistance to stretch the meaning of our faith, to turn beliefs into daily acts."
Program: Volunteers help in the soup kitchen, the shelter, community organizing, and medical work. A minimum stay of six months is preferred.
Requirements: Although no special skills are required, any skills that a volunteer has will be utilized.

Living Arrangements: Volunteers live in the shelter's staff area.
Persons with Disabilities: Volunteers with disabilities are assessed on a case-by-case basis.
Finances: Volunteers must provide their own transportation. Room and board are provided.
Deadline: None.

Community Service Volunteers

237 Pentonville Road
London N1 9NJ, England
Phone: (44-71) 278-6601

Organization: CSV is a charity which acts as a placement agency, linking potential volunteers with the projects that need them. Each year 2000 volunteers serve through CSV and over 250 of them are from outside England.
Program: Volunteers serve between four months and one year. Volunteers are generally given greater responsibility if they can serve six months or longer. Projects are located all over Great Britain. All include working face to face with people who need help. Assignments may be in residential establishments for maladjusted or disabled children or adults; in homes for ex-psychiatric patients, people with learning disabilities, or homeless people; in night shelters, working with older homeless people who may be alcoholics, addicts, or schizophrenics; in geriatric and psychiatric hospitals; in one-to-one assignments working with severely disabled individuals; in old people's homes; or on community social service teams.

Requirements: No special skills are required—"CSV rejects no one who makes a genuine offer of service."
Age: 18–35.
Finances: Volunteers pay their fare to and from London and must pay for their own accommodations during the time it takes to finalize a placement (two to four weeks) once they're in Great Britain. From within Great Britain, the fare to the project, room and board and pocket money are all provided by the agency. A placement fee of £395 is charged.
Persons with Disabilities: CSV operates a nonrejection policy. The office is fully accessible.
Deadline: A few months notice is required.
Contact: Peggy Holt, Overseas Volunteer Administrator.

"It's been a real eye opener to see the problems of some of the people of my own age. But it's good to feel that I've helped, even if it's in such a small way."

Concern/America

P.O. Box 1790
Santa Ana, CA 92702
Phone: (714) 953-8575

Organization: Concern/America is an international development and refugee aid organization, founded in California in 1972. Through the work of volunteers, Concern/America assists impoverished communities and refugees in their efforts to improve their living conditions.
Program: Volunteers, who serve for a minimum of one year, are professionals in the fields of community or-

ganizing, education, medicine, public health, and sanitation. Concern/America emphasizes training of local community members in order to impart skills and knowledge which remain with the community long after the volunteer is gone. Volunteers currently work in El Salvador, Honduras, Mexico, and Sierra Leone.
Requirements: Degree/experience in related fields. International experience helpful. Fluency in Spanish is required for all programs except Sierra Leone.
Age: Minimum 21.
Living Arrangements: Participants live in typical Third World field accommodations.
Finances: Concern/America arranges and pays for transportation to and from assignment locations. Room, board, and a small monthly stipend are provided.

Deadline: Varies from program to program.
Contact: Marianne Loewe, Director.

Covenant House

690 Eighth Avenue
New York, NY 10036
Phone: (212) 869-8946

Organization: The Covenant House Faith Community consists of Christian lay men and women who commit one year to working with the abused and runaway youth at Covenant House, living a simple lifestyle in a communal setting and praying together daily.
Program: Volunteers are needed to perform services including case management, street outreach, crisis hotline, education, health care, legal work, etc. Covenant house operates

Annarie Dennis caring for a Covenant House resident's babies.

in New York, Fort Lauderdale, New Orleans, Houston, Los Angeles, and Toronto.
Requirements: A B.A. is required in New York only. Spanish-speakers are desperately needed. Volunteers must be Christian and willing to participate in structured prayer meetings.
Age: 22–65.
Living Arrangements: Volunteers live in community.
Persons with Disabilities: Each applicant's ability to work with the residents is considered.
Finances: Room, board, and all basic necessities are provided. Volunteers also receive medical and life insurance, a monthly stipend of $12, and a stipend of $100 a month collectible at the end of the commitment.
Deadline: None.
Contact: Monika Rodman, Orientation Director, 346 West 17th Street, New York, NY 10011; (212) 921-5759.

"Working with this population of teenagers has changed my life. Suddenly, things I once felt were important become trivial in light of these kids' suffering. By helping these kids I have been able to move away from a self-centered orientation to an other-oriented outlook."

Cross-Lines Cooperative Council

1620 South 37th Street
Kansas City, KS 66106
Phone: (913) 432-5497

Organization: Cross-Lines has been working in south Kansas City since 1964, providing neighborhood services and advocacy to the community and is supported by interdenominational churches in the area. "Where people have been building barriers, Cross-Lines is building bridges."
Program: Volunteers may work for as long as they care to. In summer, groups come to volunteer; at other times, individuals are welcome. Volunteers may participate in Cross-Line's adult education program, housing repair program, an emergency assistance program, a recreation program, help in a thrift store, teach English as a second language, and work in a wood and carpentry shop.
Requirements: No special degrees are required, but experience in home repair, knowledge of academic subjects, skill in carpentry, electrical work, art, and many more fields are welcome. "A willingness to help and learn" is an important requisite.
Age: Minimum 15.
Living Arrangements: Long-term volunteers must make their own living arrangements with help from the staff. Summer groups live in a church basement.
Finances: Volunteers are fully self-supporting.
Deadline: None, except April 1 for summer groups.
Contact: Robert Moore or Judy Atwood.

CUSO

135 Rideau Street
Ottawa, Ontario
Canada K1N 9K7
Phone: (613) 563-1242

Organization: CUSO is a Canadian international development organiza-

tion involved in the placement of volunteers in the Third World.
Program: Volunteers serve for two years in Africa, Asia, Latin America, the Caribbean, and the South Pacific. They may be involved in health care, teaching, business, trades, technology, agriculture, or forestry.
Requirements: These vary with the assignment, but all volunteers must be Canadian citizens or permanent residents of Canada.
Age: No special requirements.
Living Arrangements: Volunteers live in a house or apartment, sometimes sharing facilities with other volunteers.
Persons with Disabilities: CUSO does not discriminate against people with disabilities. Each case is reviewed on an individual basis. Persons with a range of disabilities have been accommodated in the past.

Finances: Housing is generally provided. Small salary is adequate to cover overseas living costs.
Deadline: None.
Contact: Cooperant Placement.

"In a big organization, an accountant is usually stuck in one department, but here I'm dealing with the whole works. There is a lot of satisfaction in teaching accounting skills here in Zimbabwe because the people take so much interest in learning."

Daughters of Charity—Associates in Mission

7800 Natural Bridge Road
St. Louis, MO 63121
Phone: (314) 382-2800

Organization: DC—AIM is a lay volunteer program sponsored by the

A CUSO nurse at work in Papua, New Guinea

Daughters of Charity. "We challenge men and women to serve the poor and work for social justice." Volunteers serve in social work, education, childcare, computer programming, health care, and many other social and parish ministries. Assignments are for one year or more, beginning in January and August. Volunteers work in Illinois, Indiana, Louisiana, Michigan, Missouri, and Texas.
Requirements: Volunteers must be "willing to share the Vincentian way of service and ready to live simply to serve the poor." Degrees, certificates or experience required varies with the assignment, but all volunteers must have "a sense of humor, reliability and adaptability."
Age: Minimum 21.
Living Arrangements: Most volunteers live together in a house or apartment. Some live alone or with a family. Furnishings are always simple, but adequate.
Persons with Disabilities: DC—AIM is open to accepting volunteers with limited disabilities. Sites cannot always provide accommodations for those with severe disabilities. Contact us for more information.
Finances: Volunteers are provided with room and board, insurance, a stipend and travel to and from the worksite.
Deadline: None.
Contact: Ann Obernesser, Director.

"Who are the poor? In the past, the poor had only been known to me through statistics. During the last few months, these statistics have become faces, names, lives, homes, and communities."

Dental Health International

847 South Milledge Avenue
Athens, GA 30605
Phone: (404) 546-1715

Organization: DHI recruits dentists who are graduates of U.S.-accredited dental schools to work in rural areas of developing countries.
Program: DHI places dentists in Bhutan, Cameroon, Rwanda, Thailand, and the Cook Islands for limited periods of time.
Requirements: A degree in dentistry is necessary. Participants must be able to install dental equipment to turn over to host country dentists. Dentists are asked to promote flouridation and to perform water analyses to detect impurities.
Living Arrangements: Participants usually live in missionary quarters or governmental housing.
Finances: Volunteers pay their own transportation. They are asked to help locate used dental equipment for export to the project site. Room and board are provided by the host country.
Deadline: None.
Contact: Barry D. Simmons, President.

Diaconal Ministry

Deaconess Health Services
6150 Oakland Avenue
St. Louis, MO 63139
Phone: (314) 768-3890

Organization: Diaconal Ministry is a long-term voluntary service program sponsored by Deaconess Health Ser-

vices on behalf of the United Church of Christ in the greater St. Louis area.
Program: Diaconal ministers serve full-time for a minimum of one year. Their interests and skills are matched with the needs and opportunities in St. Louis area health, human service, and local church ministries. A two-week orientation and monthly nurturing sessions are part of each Diaconal minister's experience.
Requirements: Diaconal Ministry is open to mature adults, single and married, who wish to grow, have a desire to serve and are willing to explore Christian community.
Age: Minimum 21; no upper age limit.
Living Arrangements: Volunteers live together in community. A commitment to developing intentional Christian community is expected. This includes weekly meetings, shared meals, etc.
Finances: Room, food allowances, health insurance, on the job and return home travel expenses, plus a small monthly stipend are provided.
Deadline: Applications are accepted at any time. Groups begin orientation and service in January and August.
Contact: Lee W. Tyler, Coordinator.

Diocesan Lay Volunteer Program—Diocese of Salt Lake City

27 C Street
Salt Lake City, UT 84103
Phone: (801) 328-8641

Organization: The diocese includes the entire state of Utah, serving 66,000 Catholics. This diocesan office places lay volunteers in parish and diocesan apostolates.
Program: A service-oriented apostolate—where Christian witness is a goal of the volunteer and support is promised by the local church community. Most often, professional skills are brought by the volunteer into the local opportunity for service. The usual length of service is one academic year (September through May) or some other mutually agreed upon period of time. Urban and rural sites within the Diocese of Salt Lake City are available.
Requirements: Volunteers should be single Catholics who are college graduates. Spanish is sometimes helpful.
Age: College graduates.
Living Arrangements: Where possible, volunteers will live in community—and preferably with other volunteers (i.e., they will not live alone).
Finances: The volunteer is assured food, lodging, hospitalization, workman's compensation, and a monthly stipend of $200. A one-time transportation cost for travel to and from home will be reimbursed to the volunteer.
Deadline: Applications are accepted up to March 1, with a promise of a response by April 15.
Contact: Sr. Ann Mary Jurka, Director.

Dooley Foundation—Intermed USA

420 Lexington Avenue, Suite 2428
New York, NY 10170
Phone: (212) 687-3620

Organization: The Dooley Foundation—Intermed USA is a nonprofit, nonsectarian, nongovernment, nonpolitical, private voluntary organization incorporated in the State of California in 1961 with headquarters in New York City. The purpose of the Dooley Foundation is to assist Third World countries in the development of medical-care systems through self-help projects in disease prevention, health education, personnel development, and research; to provide medical aid to refugee groups; and to support and manage medical care and preventive medicine projects for primitive tribal groups.
Program: Volunteers serve for a minimum of 24 months on a variety of medical projects in Asia and Central America.
Requirements: Registered nurses, physical therapists, and medical technicians (no families) with three years experience.
Age: Minimum 25.
Living Arrangements: Housing is provided.
Finances: Staff receive room, board, travel, health insurance, and a modest stipend.
Deadline: None.
Contact: Verne Chaney, President.

East Coast Migrant Health Project

1234 Massachusetts Avenue NW
Suite 623
Washington, DC 20005
Phone: (202) 347-7377

Organization: ECMHP, sponsored by the National Migrant Workers Council, assists in the delivery of health and social services to the migrant farmworkers and their families who travel the "stream" up and down the eastern coast of the U.S. The project contracts staff with already existing health providers along the East Coast to make sure health services are available, accessible and acceptable to the migrating population. It also works to promote health education, nurturing increased health awareness, and a self-help attitude in individuals.
Program: The project is looking for nurse practitioners, community and public health nurses, licensed practical nurses, and other health professionals with specialty certificates—medical social workers, nutritionists, health educators, physician assistants, and community social service workers. Volunteers serve for at least five months. From November to May, the placements are in Florida, from June to October they are in Georgia, Maine, Maryland, New Jersey, New York, North Carolina, Pennsylvania, South Carolina, Tennessee, and Virginia.
Requirements: Besides the academic qualifications needed for the various health care positions listed above, volunteers must have "mobility (a car is a must—staff move at least twice a

year, sometimes three times), the ability to live alone and most often in rural communities, and experience in medically-underserved areas." Volunteers must be bilingual in English and either Spanish, French, or Creole-English for interviewing, instruction, and interpreting.

Age: College age and over.

Living Arrangements: Volunteers make their own living arrangements.

Finances: Volunteers receive a maintenance salary and a $ .21 per mile reimbursement for working travel.

Deadline: Volunteers should apply two months prior to availability.

Contact: Norma Rivera, Executive Director.

EIRENE

International Secretariat
Engerser Strasse 74b
D-5450 Neuwied 1
Germany

Organization: EIRENE (from the Greek word for peace) was founded in 1957 by the Historic Peace Churches (Mennonites and Brethren), the International Fellowship of Reconciliation, and European Christians actively engaged in the movement for nonviolence. It is recognized by the German government as a development aid organization and has branches in France, Germany, the Netherlands, and Switzerland.

Program: EIRENE is active in the fields of peace and development and provides partners in several countries with suitably trained and motivated volunteers. Volunteers work from one to three years in locations in Africa and Latin America, as well as in Belgium, France, Ireland, Switzerland, and the United States. Current projects include support for community-based self-help initiatives of small-scale farmers and cattle ranchers in Niger, providing primary health care in Chad, and counseling and support for agricultural cooperatives in Nicaragua.

Requirements: There are no specific requirements, but professionals are needed for some programs.

Age: Minimum 20.

Living Arrangements: Volunteers are required to live a simple lifestyle in community.

Persons with Disabilities: Depends upon the policy of partner organizations and the nature of the work.

Finances: Room and board and monthly pocket money are provided.

Episcopal Church Volunteers for Mission

Episcopal Church Center
815 Second Avenue
New York, NY 10017
Phone: (212) 922-5326

Organization: Part of the Episcopal Church, USA, Volunteers for Mission matches volunteers with projects in the U.S. and abroad.

Program: Assignments may last from six months to two years and may include teaching, social work, technology, health care, development, or theology.

Requirements: Skills must match the assignments. Candidates must be active members of their local church,

pass a physical examination, and attend orientation and training.
Age: 22–69.
Living Arrangements: Vary with project.
Finances: The volunteer's home church forms a support committee to raise funds which go directly to support the volunteer missionary while on assignment and for round-trip travel.
Deadline: None.

Food for the Hungry

7729 East Greenway Road
Scottsdale, AZ 85260
Phone: (602) 998-3100

Organization: Food for the Hungry is a nondenominational Christian relief and development organization. Its volunteer division, the International Hunger Corps, sends workers to over 20 developing countries worldwide.
Program: A number of positions are available through Food for the Hungry's Overseas Opportunities Listing, including agriculture, engineering, health care, administration, construction, education, finance, forestry, and journalism. Positions can last from one to three years, or for one's entire career.
Requirements: No particular skills are required, but many are useful. Applicants with bachelors degrees are preferred. Volunteers undergo 10 days of general orientation, five weeks of intensive pre-field training, and language training in-country.
Age: 21 to retirement age (65–70).
Living Arrangements: Vary depending on country.

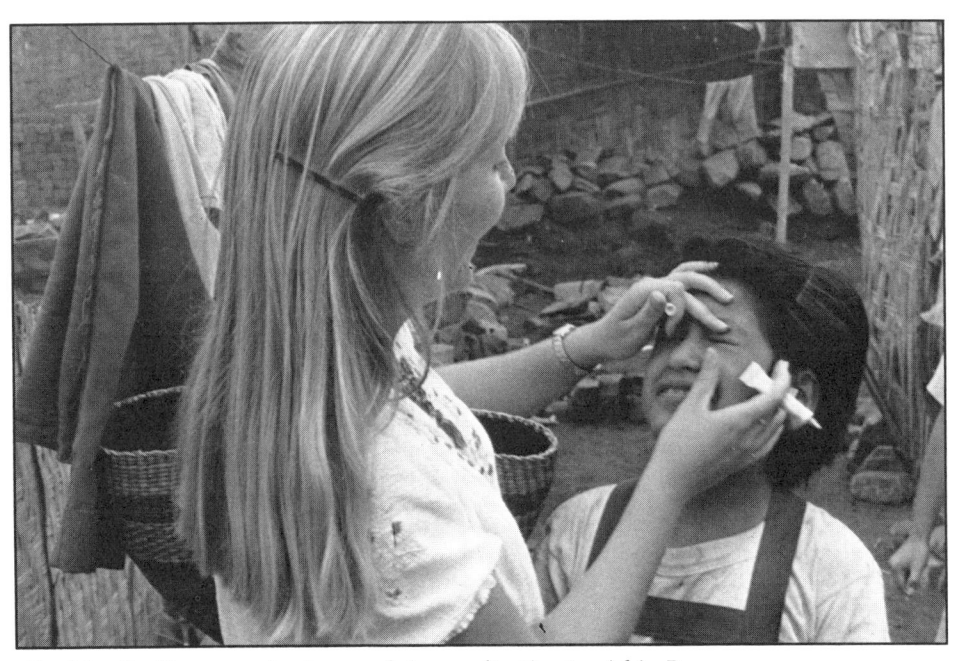

Food for the Hungry volunteer applying medication to girl in Peru.

Persons with Disabilities: Food for the Hungry accepts persons with disabilities. Extra care is taken in their overseas placement to find a suitable position.

Finances: Hunger Corps staff raise a minimum level of support determined by the specific program they enter. (Volunteers are assisted in the support-raising process.) In addition, a onetime "outbound" expense of $3,500 for singles and $6,000 for couples plus tuition for language training is required. In turn, all expenses are met, including Phase II training, transportation to and from the field, room board, insurance, monthly stipend, return stipend, etc.

Deadline: None.

Contact: Scott Allen, Recruiting Coordinator, or Gary Womelsduff, Director of Mobilization; (800) 248-6437.

"I joined Food for the Hungry because, the way the political situation is today, most of the countries of the world are closed to the traditional missionary approach."

Fourth World Movement

7600 Willow Hill Drive
Landover, MD 20785
Phone: (301) 336-9489

Organization: Founded in 1957 by Joseph Wresinki, the Movement runs cultural and educational projects in partnership with extremely poor families in 22 countries on five continents based on the conviction: "Wherever men and women are condemned to live in extreme poverty, human rights are violated. It is our solemn duty to come together to ensure that they are respected."

Program: Long-term service commitments of at least two years begin with a two-month internship in the U.S. Service may include educational activities with children, manual work, office work, and research. Internship periods begin in January, March, June, and October.

Requirements: Prospective volunteers must be high school graduates with at least two additional years of education or work experience.

Age: Minimum 19.

Living Arrangements: Volunteers live in individual rooms but prepare meals together.

Finances: Housing is provided. After the first month, a weekly stipend is provided. This covers more than the cost of groceries. Living allowances vary according to the country. Insurance is provided upon completion of the two-month internship. There is an application fee of $25, returned if the applicant is turned down.

Deadline: Write three months ahead for summer and fall internships..

Contact: Send a stamped, business-length envelope to Susan Devins, Director.

"Community life and the necessity of being aware of each other's needs teaches volunteers a sensitivity that extends to their contact with the poorest."

Franciscan Outreach Association

1645 West LeMoyne Street
Chicago, IL 60622
Phone: (312) 278-6724

Organization: An independent non-profit organization that places Catholic lay people in service in the U.S. in the spirit of St. Francis.
Program: Assignments ordinarily last one year and include, in the U.S., providing services to the urban poor, assisting with shelters, soup kitchens, an AIDS program, and a halfway house for ex-offenders. In 1983, over 300 volunteers served.
Requirements: "Good character, maturity, and a sense of commitment."
Age: Minimum 18.
Living Arrangements: Volunteers live in community and participate in daily prayer and mass.
Persons with Disabilities: Everyone is welcome as long as they can do the job.
Finances: Room, board, medical coverage, and a small stipend are provided.
Deadline: None.
Contact: Fr. Albert Merz, Executive Director.

Friends of the Third World

National Resource Center
611 West Wayne Street
Fort Wayne, IN 46802
Phone: (219) 422-6821

Organization: Friends of the Third World is concerned with domestic and international hunger and poverty; to combat them, it provides alternative markets for Third World crafts and Nicaraguan coffee, distributes books and educational materials to churches, schools, and community groups, and advises local volunteer groups on activities such as hunger walks, World Food Day celebrations, peace education, etc.
Program: Volunteers are asked to serve for at least six months. Positions may be available in El Paso, Texas; Fort Wayne, Indiana; Los Angeles, California; and Phoenix, Arizona. Volunteer assignments include publicity work, recycling, coffee shipping, work in a craft shop, printing, community organizing and research. "We look on our program as an opportunity for individuals to learn while taking positive action toward social change, especially in the areas of public education about hunger and poverty."
Requirements: "We prefer those who have graduated from high school or an equivalent and have had some experience working in some type of anti-poverty organization or cooperative organization. Helpful skills would be foreign language ability (French or Spanish), international experience in Third World countries, graphic arts and bookkeeping skills. We can train those willing to learn and work as part of a team."
Age: Minimum 18.
Living Arrangements: Volunteers may live with area families or, in Fort Wayne, in the Resource Center in a private room, sharing kitchen facilities and household duties with other volunteers.

Persons with Disabilities: Applications from persons with disabilities are welcomed.
Finances: Room, board, and a weekly stipend are provided.
Deadline: Two weeks to two months before assignment begins.
Contact: James F. Goetsch, Administrative Coordinator.

Habitat for Humanity

419 West Church Street
Americus, GA 31709
Phone: (912) 924-6935

Organization: Habitat is an ecumenical Christian housing ministry which works together with the poor to build low-cost housing they can purchase at no profit and no interest. Habitat works in the U.S. and abroad. Their motto: "Building in partnership with God's people in need."
Program: There are over 600 Habitat projects currently in operation in the U.S and Canada. Around the world, over 60 projects are operating in 29 developing countries. Thousands of volunteers participate each year. At the international headquarters in Americus, volunteers serve for periods of 10 weeks to a year or longer. Volunteers are involved in construction, administration, clerical work, data processing, fund raising, public relations, bookkeeping, accountancy, typing, graphic arts, childcare, and more. At affiliate projects in North America, many of the above skills are required. Volunteers from the local community may serve, giving a few hours per week or a weekend of service, and volunteers from other areas may come to serve for longer periods. Overseas assignments are for three years, which includes a training period in Americus. Overseas volunteers use construction, administrative, and bookkeeping skills and must have a "willingness to share life in another culture."
Requirements: Habitat welcomes people of all faiths for U.S. service, but it is a Christian organization which openly proclaims a spiritual basis in the "economics of Jesus." While Habitat does need individuals to bring specific skills to this ministry, anyone with a willingness to learn and to serve is welcome to apply.
Age: Minimum 18 for international headquarters; 21 for overseas volunteers. Individual projects in the U.S. and Canada either set their own age limits or have none.
Living Arrangements: In Americus, volunteers share houses in a residential neighborhood. In the U.S. and Canada, housing may or may not be provided, depending on the project. Overseas volunteers live in houses similar to those they build.
Persons with Disabilities: Persons with disabilities are welcome to work at the Habitat Headquarters. However, the facilities are such that accessibility might be difficult.
Finances: At international headquarters, volunteers receive a weekly food stipend as well as housing, utilities, cleaning supplies, and laundry facilities. Each U.S. and Canadian project sets its own policy. Overseas volunteers receive a monthly stipend, housing and major medical coverage. They are expected to fundraise.

Deadline: None.
Contact: Volunteer Services.

"The volunteers are building more than houses, they are building the beginnings of new lives for children, youth, and adults."

Health Volunteers Overseas

c/o Washington Station
P.O. Box 65157
Washington, DC 20035-5157
Phone: (202) 296-0928

Organization: HVO is a nonprofit, private organization formed to "upgrade, broaden, and strengthen the skills of health professionals in developing countries." The aim of HVO is to build an "ongoing capability in developing countries that will benefit the population long after the volunteers have departed."

Program: HVO recruits volunteers from a range of health disciplines. At present there are five divisions—anesthesia, dentistry, general surgery, oral and maxillofacial surgery, and orthopedics—operating in Bangladesh, Bhutan, China, Egypt, Ethiopia, Grenada, India, Indonesia, Jamaica, Malawi, Mexico, Mozambique, Pakistan, St. Lucia, Transkei, Trinidad, and Uganda. The emphasis is on training and the use of technology. HVO volunteers serve for four to six weeks although longer term service may be arranged.

Requirements: Most volunteers are licensed, board certified/board eligible medical doctors, registered nurses, physical therapists, dentists, and dental hygienists.

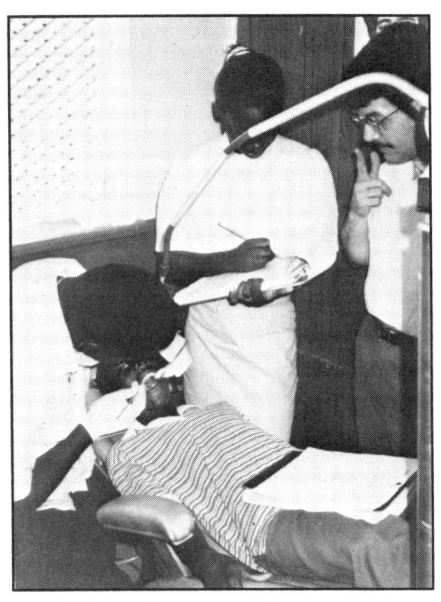

Health Volunteers Overseas participants teach dentistry techniques.

Age: No minimum or maximum.
Living Arrangements: This varies from program to program but may involve a room at a hospital, a local guest house, or hotel.
Finances: In some cases, room and board are provided. Volunteers must pay their own travel expenses, and there is a $100 annual membership fee. Members receive regular updates on volunteer opportunities.
Deadline: None.
Contact: Kate Skillman, Program Coordinator

"One valuable asset in a volunteer is equanimity and the realization that one cannot transplant United States patterns of care in a short time frame. Changes in the system require time and patience and recognition that 'correcting' a problem may not have a desireable end result."

Helen Keller International

15 West 16th Street
New York, NY 10011
Phone: (212) 807-5800

Organization: HKI was founded in 1915 to help soldiers blinded in the First World War return to normal lives. HKI's primary goal is to prevent blindness and rehabilitate those who are already blind. The agency works entirely in Third World countries.
Program: Periodically, positions are available for health-care professionals—ophthalmologists, ophthalmic nurses, public health planners, epidemiologists, nutritionists, training specialists, physicians, and rehabilitation field workers. Country directors and consultants serve from two weeks to two years providing technical assistance to prevent blindness, to rehabilitate those who are blind, and to train local personnel to carry on in the self-help tradition after HKI teams depart.
Requirements: Participants must have the appropriate degrees and skills for their professions. Usually only English is required, but fluency in the language of the host country may be necessary.
Finances: Room and board are provided in some cases.
Deadline: None.
Contact: Personnel Director.

Human Service Alliance

3983 Old Greensboro Road
Winston-Salem, NC 27101
Phone: (919) 761-8745

Organization: The Human Service Alliance is a nonprofit human service organization that provides respite care for developmentally disabled persons, care for the terminally ill, mediation (conflict resolution), and health and wellness support at its Care for the Terminally Ill Center. The Center offers a home-like setting where the guests live out their lives in a loving and supportive environment.
Program: Every aspect of the Center's operation is staffed by volunteers, so you can contribute in any number of ways. One role is caring directly for the guests, much as a loving family member would: keeping them company, helping with their grooming, reading to them, or simply holding hands. In addition to direct care, there are other equally important functions like cooking, housekeeping, gardening and grounds maintenance, typing, computer work, and much more. Both long- and short-term volunteers are needed.
Requirements: No prior special training is needed.
Age: Volunteers can be any age.
Living Arrangements: There are a number of comfortable rooms for full-time, live-in volunteers. During free time, Winston-Salem offers a wide variety of activities.
Persons with Disabilities: Persons with disabilities are encouraged to apply.

Finances: Volunteers are provided with room and board.
Deadline: None.
Contact: Christa Danziger, Volunteer Team.

"When you help make the final days of someone's life the best they can be, you transform your own life in the process."

Innisfree

Route 2, Box 506
Crozet, VA 22932
Phone: (804) 823-5400

Organization: Innisfree is a self-contained working community for adults with mental disabilities, built on 600 acres of rolling farmland adjacent to the Shenandoah National Forest, 17 miles from Charlottesville, Virginia. Fifty residents live in eight households which are shared by houseparents, single co-workers, and the handicapped residents. Bread, granola, hand-woven fabrics and wood-work items from the Village are all sold to nearby communities and at craft fairs. "The rationale is that growth comes at a pace natural and therapeutic for the individual within a supportive environment."
Program: Volunteers must commit themselves to at least one year of service. There's a one-month trial period with an evaluation at the end to determine mutual compatibility. Volunteers serve as houseparents, sharing in household chores, cooking, cleaning, and informal counseling, and also participating in the weavery, bakery, workshop, or garden.
Requirements: No special skills are required, but volunteers must possess an interest in living with the disabled; patience, common sense, ability to empathize, a sense of humor and resourcefulness are other desirable qualities. Interest in "community process and in living in a rural setting is essential."
Age: Minimum 21.
Living Arrangements: Volunteers live in a house with 3 to 14 other people, usually two volunteer coworkers and four handicapped.
Finances: Room and board, a monthly stipend of $150, a vacation allowance, medical expenses, and a $45 per month accumulating severance fund are provided.
Deadline: None.
Contact: Recruitment Desk. (Personal visits are strongly recommended. Visiting arrangements must be made in advance.)

"Innisfree Village is precisely that—a village, a community of handicapped and nonhandicapped adults sharing a common life."

International Christian Youth Exchange

Voluntary Service Program
134 West 26th Street
New York, NY 10001
Phone: (212) 206-7307

Organization: ICYE is an international, intercultural organization composed of autonomous national committees in 32 countries. In the U.S., ICYE is divided into regional teams which plan and carry out programs for U.S. exchangees going abroad, exchangees spending their year in the U.S., and host families. The national program staff is based in New York City, with an area office in Northern California. ICYE began as a bilateral exchange program with Germany in 1949, and in 1957 branched out to include more countries.

Program: Exchangees live in any of 32 countries of Africa, Asia, Eastern and Western Europe, Latin America, Australia, and New Zealand. Service may include assisting in a drug rehabilitation program in Italy, working with a womens' rights organization in Mexico, helping to establish an Independent Living Program for the physically disabled in Japan or working with "guest workers" in Germany as an outgrowth of interest in minority immigrant issues. "The possibilities are as varied as the interest and skills of the exchangee." If participants are of high school age, they attend high school, participate in extracurricular activities along with their foreign counterparts, and have an opportunity to perform voluntary service in the community in which they are living. This service may include work with children, the elderly, the disabled, or with environmental groups. Older exchangees may live independently while doing their voluntary service. Exchangees begin their year of participation in late July with an orientation in this country before departure.

Requirements: "The adjustments required in an international exchange experience demand adaptability, resourcefulness, maturity, integrity, common sense, convictions and stability."

Age: 16–30; on occasion older participants are considered.

Living Arrangements: Volunteers live with a host family or on their own depending on their age and interests.

Persons with Disabilities: All positions are open to persons with physical disabilities. Placements are generally accessible. ICYE has developed a handbook for participation by persons with disabilities.

Finances: Fee for participation is $4,400 which includes room, board, international travel costs, insurance, orientation, and three conferences per year. Some scholarship aid is available.

Deadline: November 15 (Late applications accepted through April 15 on a space-available basis.)

Contact: Outbound Programs.

"Obviously I've learned a lot of practical things about working with disabled people not to mention 100% more Swedish than I knew five months ago. But what I value the most is a new appreciation of laughter and humor."

International Eye Foundation

7801 Norfolk Avenue
Bethesda, MD 20814
Phone: (301) 986-1830

Organization: Founded in 1961, IEF works for "the promotion of peace through the prevention and cure of blindness worldwide."

Program: One aspect of IEF's work is to send certified ophthalmologists to Africa, the Caribbean, and Latin America to teach and to provide

therapeutic services. Volunteers serve from 2 to 26 weeks.
Requirements: Participants must be certified ophthalmologists.
Finances: Volunteers pay their own expenses.
Contact: Edwin M. Henderson, Administrative Director.

International Liaison of Lay Volunteers in Mission

U.S. Catholic Network Center of Lay Mission Programs
4121 Harewood Road NE
Washington, DC 20017
Phone: (800) 543-5046

Organization: ILLVIM is the official center for the U.S. Catholic Church's promotion, referral, and recruitment of lay mission volunteers in the U.S. and overseas.
Program: ILLVIM is a clearinghouse for lay volunteer programs. In its annual publication, *Response*, are listed over 145 programs which offer opportunities for three weeks to three years of service in the U.S., and two to three years of service abroad. Most groups welcome Christians from all denominations; some accept only Catholics. At present over 4,500 lay volunteers are serving through ILLVIM's 145 lay volunteer programs. *Response* is available upon request, as is consultative advice concerning programs and referral service for potential volunteers. An annual conference as well as periodic information seminars are open to all.
Contact: Sr. Ellen Cavanaugh, Executive Director.

"I won't say that it takes a special person to do lay volunteer work, but it takes a different kind of person. You have to be more adventuresome and willing to take some risks for what you believe in."

International Lifeline

Box 32714
Oklahoma City, OK 73123-0914
Phone: (405) 728-2828

Organization: In operation for over 10 years, this organization offers medical volunteers an opportunity to serve in Rwanda and Togo.
Program: Working in conjunction with local government health centers and hospitals, International Lifeline provides volunteers, vaccines, medicine, and equipment.
Requirements: Volunteers must have medical degrees and licenses in the field appropriate to their assignment. All volunteers must be willing to serve alongside or under supervision of local physicians and officials.
Living Arrangements: Volunteers will stay in hotels or housing approved by International Lifeline.
Finances: Participants are required to pay all expenses.
Deadline: Thirty days before departure.
Contact: Robert E. Watkins, President.

International Rescue Committee

386 Park Avenue South
New York, NY 10016
Phone: (212) 679-0010

Organization: IRC/Overseas Programs is devoted to helping refugees who escape from religious, racial, and political persecution in their countries. Uprooted victims of war and famine are also assisted by IRC. Founded in 1933 at the request of Albert Einstein, to help anti-Nazis escaping from Hitler's Germany, IRC now has relief and settlement programs for refugees from Afghanistan, Cambodia, Ethiopia, Laos, Mozambique, and other countries.

Program: Volunteers serve for a minimum of six months, teaching English as a second language to refugees in Peshawar, Pakistan.

Requirements: ESL or curriculum development experience is required.
Age: Minimum 20.
Living Arrangements: Volunteers usually live in group houses.
Finances: Volunteers receive a monthly stipend and housing.
Deadline: None.
Contact: Liliana M. Keith, Recruiter, Overseas Programs.

International Voluntary Services

1424 16th Street NW, Suite 204
Washington, DC 20036
Phone: (202) 387-5533

Organization: IVS is a private, non-profit organization which provides technical assistance volunteers in small-scale rural development projects in the Third World.

Class at Lycée Malalai, a school for girls in Peshawar served by the International Rescue Committee.

Program: Volunteers serve a minimum of two years, in the fields of agriculture, small business/cooperative development, public health, and technology in Bangladesh, Bolivia, Ecuador, and Zimbabwe.
Requirements: Volunteers must have at least two years previous experience working in the Third World at the grassroots level. No exceptions to this rule are made. A degree in a relevant field is required. For Latin America assignments, fluent Spanish is required, for Francophone Africa, fluent French is a prerequisite. In other locations, volunteers learn the language on arrival.
Persons with Disabilities: "IVS does not discriminate."
Finances: Stipend, a cost of living allowance, housing, transportation, insurance, and an education allowance for children in primary and secondary school are provided.
Deadline: None.
Contact: Recruitment Office.

Interns for Peace

270 West 89th Street, Room 201
New York, NY 10024
Phone: (212) 580-0540

Organization: For 15 years, IFP has been dedicated to "building understanding, trust and respect between Jewish and Arab citizens of Israel." IFP trains and then places community workers to live and work in paired Jewish/Arab communities in developing cooperative projects that benefit both groups.
Program: Internships begin in the fall each year and involve a commitment of at least two years (this includes a month-long training period on a kibbutz before entering the field). Interns work on projects that have been developed by IFP and community residents. IFP only works in communities that show their commitment to the program; the participation of the village is basic to the philosophy of IFP. Projects are designed to meet community needs and are meant to provide ongoing structures to serve the village long after the intern has moved on.
Requirements: Interns must have a B.A. or an equivalent degree. A previous stay in Israel of six months (minimum) and fluency in either Hebrew or Arabic, as well as experience in either community or person-to-person work are necessary background for our most effective interns, who then learn the alternate language in order to work within both cultures. Interns must be either Arab or Jewish, and marital status is not important.
Age: Must be a college graduate.
Living Arrangements: Interns live in the Arab or Jewish community in which they work in a group house or an apartment.
Finances: Most communities provide housing and utilities; volunteers receive a monthly stipend sufficient to cover all expenses.
Deadline: Applications accepted continously throughout the year.

"I see the program as a good way to contribute to the way I would like Israel to be."

Jesuit Volunteer Corps

East
Eighteenth & Thompson Streets
Philadelphia, PA 19121
Phone: (215) 232-0300
Midwest
P.O. Box 32692
Detroit, MI 48232
Phone: (313) 894-1140
Northwest
P.O. Box 3928
Portland, OR 97208-3928
Phone: (503) 228-2457
Southwest
P.O. Box 23404
Oakland, CA 94623-9991
Phone: (415) 465-5016
South
P.O. Box 3126
Houston, TX 77253-3126
Phone: (713) 223-5387

Organization: JVC began in 1956 in Copper Valley, Alaska, and has since expanded throughout the U.S. It is a Christian organization of "motivated, mature, adaptable men and women who work with people who are poor and oppressed and with organizations and individuals committed to the realization of social justice."
Program: Volunteers serve for one year, beginning in mid-August; if they wish to stay on, they may. JVC participants may work as teachers, community organizers, day-care workers, paralegal assistants, nurses, occupational and physical therapists, parish assistants, campus ministers, village workers, recreation directors, counselors, "skid-row" workers, etc. JVC places hundreds of volunteers in projects each year. Some examples: One volunteer works at a center in Detroit helping battered women and their children seek out legal counsel, find a new place to live and deal with other immediate problems; another, in Milwaukee, works with senior citizens, leading activities, serving as advocate, running errands, etc; and a volunteer in a very poor neighborhood in Chicago works at an emergency food pantry.
Requirements: Most positions require a college degree. Some call for work experience, but others, such as cook or dormitory supervisor do not.
Age: Minimum 21.
Living Arrangements: JVC emphasizes a simple life style, where "people rather than things are valued." Volunteers live in groups of five to seven, usually in the community in which they work. An integral part of the JVC experience is "the opportunity to build a reflective community that encourages the development and growth of a faith identity."
Persons with Disabilities: The nature of the work and the inner city living arrangements preclude some major disabilities. However, efforts are made to include participation by persons with disabilities.
Finances: Volunteers receive a stipend which covers room and board, medical insurance, travel home at the end of the year, and an additional monthly stipend for personal expenses.
Deadline: None.
Contact: Call or write to the regional office closest to the area in which you'd like to work.

Jubilee Partners

P.O. Box 68
Comer, GA 30629
Phone: (404) 783-5131

Organization: Jubilee is a Christian service community dedicated to the service of the poor and to peace education.
Program: Service opportunities are open to Christians and non-Christians to work with refugees in Comer, Georgia. Volunteers may participate from January to May, June to July, or September to December (extensions are possible). Opportunities include teaching English to refugees, gardening, construction, and office work.
Requirements: Participants must be flexible—willing to do whatever needs to be done. There are usually 15 openings.
Age: Minimum 18.
Living Arrangements: Most volunteers live in the nine-bedroom guest house, but a few live in other houses with resident members.
Persons with Disabilities: Each application is looked at individually. The policy is nondiscriminatory, but facilities would not lend themselves well to certain needs, e.g., rough terrain probably not wheelchair accessible.
Finances: Participants arrange and pay for their own transportation. Room and board and a stipend of $10 a week are provided.
Deadline: None.
Contact: Josie Winterfeld, Volunteer Coordinator.

Lalmba Association

7685 Quartz Street
Golden, CO 80403
Phone: (303) 420-1810

Organization: Lalmba has been at work in Africa for 29 years under the guidance of a Colorado-based couple, Hugh and Marty Downey. At present, the organization operates three clinics in Sudan and one in Kenya as well as a number of what they call "branch clinics" and an orphanage. Lalmba recently opened a home in Mexico for abandoned children.
Program: Volunteers are doctors, nurses, technicians, and administrative personnel. At times, construction workers and teachers are also needed. The minimum commitment is one year; two to three years is preferable. Volunteers attend orientation in Colorado.
Requirements: Physicians and registered nurses qualify.
Age: 25–55.
Living Arrangements: Volunteers live "in very nice grass huts."
Persons with Disabilities: Applications from those with disabilities are encouraged.
Finances: Pocket money, transportation, and room and board are provided during the term of service.
Deadline: None.
Contact: Marty Downey, Medical Director.

"God's loving gift to us is life. I feel an urgency to use it helping our fellow man."

L'Arche Mobile

151 South Ann Street
Mobile, AL 36604
Phone: (205) 438-2094

Organization: L'Arche Mobile is an ecumenical Christian community where mentally disabled people live together as a family with non-disabled people. L'Arche Mobile is a permanent member of the International Federation of L'Arche, begun in France in 1964.
Program: L'Arche Mobile creates a homelike environment for persons with mental disabilities. Most residents come from state institutions where they have had little contact with their own families. A Day/Work Program focuses on the needs and abilities of each person. Typical projects include activities such as arts and crafts, yard work, and baking. Each person's schedule combines exercise with accomplishing goals in the workplace.
Requirements: None.
Age: Minimum 18.
Living Arrangements: Volunteers live in private rooms, with a separate apartment available for days off.
Persons with Disabilities: Persons with disabilities are accepted. Housing is accessible.
Finances: Volunteers receive room, board, insurance, and, after the first month, $325 a month.
Deadline: None.
Contact: Martin E. O'Malley, Director.

Leonard Cheshire Foundation

26-29 Maunsel Street
London SW1P 2QN
England

Organization: This charity runs 83 homes throughout the United Kingdom. There are also 180 homes in 48 other countries.
Program: Volunteers are needed for three months to one year as care assistants in homes for severely disabled adults. Most homes are in rural locations throughout the U.K.
Requirements: Academic qualifications are not essential, but volunteers must be responsible, hardworking, punctual, and willing to undertake a wide variety of tasks.
Age: 18–30.
Living Arrangements: Volunteers live in the home they are working in, perhaps sharing a room with one other person.
Persons with Disabilities: Because of the nature of the work caring for persons with disabilities, volunteers must be fit and able-bodied.
Finances: Room and board and a small stipend are provided.
Deadline: None.
Contact: Personnel Secretary.

Lutheran Volunteer Corps

1226 Vermont Avenue NW
Washington, DC 20005
Phone: (202) 387-3222

Organization: LVC is a service program based on the ideals of working for social justice, living in Christian community, and exploring a simplified lifestyle. A direct ministry of Lutheran Place Memorial Church in Washington, D.C., LVC began as a response to the needs of the inner city. Since its beginning 12 years ago, the program has expanded to Baltimore, Chicago, Milwaukee, Minneapolis-Saint Paul, and Wilmington, Delaware.

Program: Volunteers serve for one year (beginning at the end of August) or longer. Opportunities include working directly with people who are homeless, hungry, elderly, or otherwise needy. Placements are also available within the public policy, advocacy, and community organizing sector. All positions are full time and carry major responsibility.

Requirements: LVC seeks commitment, flexibility, energy, and responsibility in its volunteers. LVC is an ecumenical program and welcomes people from diverse age, racial, and faith backgrounds.

Age: Minimum 21, but there is no upper limit—the oldest volunteer to date is 70.

Living Arrangements: Volunteers live together in communities of four to seven. Commitment to maintaining community is expected, which may include "community nights," shared meals, and other activities.

Persons with Disabilities: Applications from those with disabilities are reviewed on a case by case basis. No facilities are currently wheelchair accessible.

Finances: Room and board, health insurance, travel expenses plus a small monthly stipend are provided. Student loans are deferable.

Deadline: Applications are available in January and placements are made between May 15 and July 30. As placements fill quickly, interested people are encouraged to apply as early as possible.

Contact: Don Billen, Program Assistant.

Lutheran World Mission Volunteers

Evangelical Lutheran Church in America
8765 West Higgins Road
Chicago, IL 60631-4192
Phone: (312) 380-2631

Organization: LWMV is a program of the Evangelical Lutheran Church in America Division for Global Mission.

Program: LWMV is essentially a match-making service. It puts potential volunteers in touch with projects that require lay mission volunteers. LWMV matches skilled volunteers who want to serve from two months to two years in such countries as: Cameroon, Liberia, Madagascar, Nepal, Papua New Guinea, Tanzania, and Zimbabwe. Volunteers who have served recently have included accountants, administrators, agriculturalists, auto mechanics, builders, childcare workers, health care providers, librarians, and computer programmers.

Requirements: Appropriate professional degrees are usually required. For some assignments, fluent Spanish or French is necessary. "Most invitations expect that volunteers are committed Christians."

Age: No set requirements.
Living Arrangements: Housing varies from site to site.
Finances: Volunteers must pay their own transportation and their own living expenses. "Many volunteers have funded their service entirely from personal resources. Others have gotten assistance from families and friends and, still others have been helped by their home congregation."
Deadline: None.
Contact: Jack F. Reents, Director.

Marianist Voluntary Service Communities

P.O. Box 9224
Wright Brothers Branch
Dayton, OH 45409
Phone: (513) 229-4630/3287

Organization: MVSC places Christian men and women in agencies in urban areas of the U.S. Emphasis is given to community living and service to the disadvantaged.
Program: Volunteers may do teaching, nursing, community organizing, youth or crisis shelter work, counseling work with the mentally and physically handicapped and with senior citizens. Terms of service are one to two years and usually begin in early August. MVSC communities are located in Cincinnati, Cleveland, and Dayton, Ohio; Covington, Kentucky; and Queens, New York.
Requirements: Necessary skills vary, but everyone must have an "ability to be open and flexible in living arrangements and must be open to negotiation with others."

Age: Minimum 20.
Living Arrangements: Volunteers live together in groups of three to six people. They pray together, share meals and other activities. Participants may be single or married without dependants.
Persons with Disabilities: MVSC places priority on ability to live effectively in community as well as to give service. Each applicant is considered on an individual basis.
Finances: Volunteers receive a monthly allowance which is enough to cover their room and board and other expenses.
Deadline: None, program begins every year in mid-August.
Contact: Laura Libertore, Director.

"The volunteer year was rewarding, challenging, and fun—a growth-filled, great experience. And I would do it again. Being back in the classroom, I find that I am relating some of my volunteer experiences to the theories I learn in sociology."

Maryknoll Lay Missioners

Maryknoll, NY 10545
Phone: (914) 762-6364

Organization: Maryknoll Lay Missioners is a part of the Catholic Foreign Mission Society of America. It has been placing volunteers in missions abroad for the past 16 years.
Program: Lay missioners serve for three and a half years. Two orientation sessions (spring and fall) are offered during odd years; during even years only fall orientation is offered. Participants may be placed in Bolivia,

Brazil, Chile, Guatemala, Hong Kong, Israel, Japan, Kenya, Korea, Nicaragua, Taiwan, Tanzania, Thailand, Venezuela, and various countries in the Middle East. They may be involved in pastoral work, health care, adult education, agriculture, community organizing, special education, youth work, or communications.

Requirements: All lay missioners must have at least one year experience in their field of specialization. They must be Roman Catholic and have experience working with a U.S. Church. Language training is provided overseas.

Age: The average age is 23–40.

Living Arrangements: "Simple but adequate."

Finances: Room, board, and travel expenses are provided.

Deadline: Applications for the spring orientation program are due July 31 of the preceding year. Applications for the fall program are due January 31 of the same year.

Contact: Kathy Wright.

Mendenhall Ministries

309 Center Street
P.O. Box 368
Mendenhall, MS 39114
Phone: (601) 847-3421

Organization: Mendenhall Ministries is a nonprofit Christian organization whose purpose is to minister to the needs of the poor in rural areas of Mississippi and to develop models by which Christians can respond to the needs of the poor. The organization operates a thrift store, cooperative health care center, adult education center, cooperative farm, community law office, leadership development program, recreation center, and nursery and elementary school.

Program: Volunteers are needed to teach, tutor, farm, do legal research, paralegal work, maintenance, construction, secretarial work, accounting, recreation leadership, disciple leadership, writing, and photography. Opportunities are available year-round for any length of service.

Requirements: Special skills or degrees are not required but are helpful.

Living Arrangements: Volunteers usually share small apartments.

Finances: Volunteers must pay their own food and transportation expenses. Accommodation is available for $40 per week.

Deadline: None.

Contact: Antonio McKinnis, Volunteer Coordinator.

Mennonite Board of Missions

Box 370
Elkhart, IN 46515-0370
Phone: (219) 294-7523

Organization: The Board's Voluntary Service program supports volunteers who are involved in community development and the establishment of healthy neighborhood relationships in various locations throughout the United States. "The purpose is to be a visible demonstration of the good news of the kingdom of God."

Program: Volunteers serve for two or more years in urban and rural areas of Arizona, California, Colorado, Washington, D.C., Illinois, Maryland, Mississippi, New York, Pennsylvania, Texas, and Virginia. The areas of service include administrative and business management, community social work, education, health care, home repair and construction, leadership training, and peace and justice advocacy. All volunteers participate in a week-long orientation which includes an introduction to the program, perspectives on working with the poor and the theological basis for service.
Requirements: Some positions require special degrees or certification; positions are designed to match the skills of the volunteer. Spanish proficiency is helpful in many placements. The program is open "to all persons who view service as an outgrowth of Christian commitment."
Age: Minimum 20.
Living Arrangements: Volunteers live in households with four to six other volunteers, sharing household tasks.
Persons with Disabilities: MBM accepts volunteers who are able to fulfill assignment requirements, and would make special efforts to facilitate the placement of a qualified person with disabilities.
Finances: Participants receive a small monthly stipend.
Deadline: None.
Contact: Berni Kaufman, Recruitment Manager.

Mennonite Central Committee

21 South 12th Street
Akron, PA 17501-0500
Phone: (717) 859-1151

Organization: MCC is the cooperative relief and service agency of North American Mennonite and Brethren in Christ church conferences.
Program: Volunteers serve for two years in North America or three years overseas (there are opportunities in 50 countries around the world). MCC volunteers may be involved in projects involving agriculture, health, education, social services, or community development.
Requirements: For most assignments, two years of college are required; for some, four or more. Language training is normally offered as part of the preservice training. Volunteers must be members of a Christian church.
Age: Minimum 21.
Living Arrangements: Accommodations tend to vary but "can be quite rustic."
Persons with Disabilities: Since 1986 MCC has had a project to integrate persons with disabilities as volunteers into its programs in developing countries.
Finances: Room and board and a monthly stipend are provided.
Deadline: Varies with the assignment.
Contact: Bill Loewen, Secretary for Personnel Services.

Mennonite Voluntary Service

722 Main Street, Box 347
Newton, KS 67114
Phone: (316) 283-5100

Organization: MVS is one of the service arms of the General Conference Mennonite Church dedicated to helping meet the needs of poor and disadvantaged people in North America. "It attempts to match human resources to human needs in obedience to Christ. MVS also works to change oppressive social structures."

Program: MVS volunteers serve in any of 30 communities in the U.S. and Canada, in big cities, small towns and isolated outposts. Most volunteers serve for two years but shorter assignments may be available. Openings are listed in a bulletin that MVS issues periodically. Some of the possibilities include the fields of childcare, community development, education, health care, housing rehabilitation, legal aid, mental health, native ministries, nutrition, peace and justice, prison ministry, office work, senior citizen services, social services, and youth services. Specific examples taken from a recent bulletin of approximately 100 opportunities are: preschool teachers at an inner city school, woman's advocate in a shelter for abused women, teachers at an elementary school on a Hopi Reservation, director of an emergency assistance center, teachers of English for refugees, and so on. Most urgent needs include housing rehabilitation workers, social workers, secretaries, and peace activists.

Requirements: Some positions require advanced professional training; others are open to high school graduates with no special training or experience. Spanish is helpful for some assignments. "Volunteers in MVS are encouraged to be part of a local congregation and to join the search for a faithful life and ministry."

Age: Minimum 18.

Living Arrangements: MVS volunteers live cooperatively in households of 3 to 12 people, sharing decision making, mutual support and household responsibilities. "In a society pushing material accumulation and individualism...MVS calls people into another way of life...a shared, simple life style, mutual caring and sharing..."

Persons with Disabilities: MVS tries to make placement decisions based upon abilities, not disabilities. Arrangements for participation are made on individual basis.

Finances: Room and board, travel to and from the assignment, and health care are covered; a monthly personal allowance is provided as well. Assistance with educational loans and other benefits are offered.

Deadline: None.

Contact: Kristen Mayhue, Personnel Director.

"I have learned just enough about social issues, poverty, prejudice, etc., that I can not go back to the same life I left. I am seeking a similar job and hope to be involved in these issues from now on. I feel so much more alive!"

Mercy Corps

Gwynedd Mercy College
Gwynedd Valley, PA 19437
Phone: (215) 641-5535

Organization: The Corps is an association of men and women who "respond in faith to the call of mercy to serve God's people, especially the poor, the sick and the uneducated." It has been operating since 1979.
Program: Volunteers serve for one year beginning in August with a week-long orientation at Gwynedd Mercy College. Participants serve throughout the United States. They may work as social workers, teachers, health care workers, group home parents, ministers for the elderly, recreational directors, parish workers, etc. Each April the Corps publishes a placement list, enumerating the areas in need of volunteers.
Requirements: Corps members need to have the necessary credentials for their assignment and a strong desire to serve. They must be "flexible, adaptable, have a sense of humor and feel commitment to the Church."
Age: Minimum 21.
Living Arrangements: Volunteers live together in in lodgings provided by the apostolic agency with which they work. Most have private rooms.
Persons with Disabilities: MC accepts persons with disabilities depending on the service site.
Finances: Room and board, a stipend, transportation to and from the place of service, and medical insurance are provided.
Deadline: June 1.
Contact: Sr. Kathleen Lyons, Director.

Mercy Corps International

3030 S.W. First Avenue
Portland, OR 97201
Phone: (503) 242-1032

Organization: Mercy Corps International is a Christian relief development organization, focusing on agriculture, housing, and medicine.
Program: Volunteers are needed to work in agricultural and medical clinics in underdeveloped countries around the world for at least one year.
Requirements: Skills vary according to the assignment, but general agricultural and medical skills are needed.
Age: Minimum 18.
Living Arrangements: Volunteers share quarters.
Finances: Room and board, insurance, and a monthly stipend of $1,000 are provided.
Deadline: None.
Contact: Sandy Fitzgerald, Personnel Coordinator.

Mission Volunteers/USA

Presbyterian Church (USA)
100 Witherspoon Street
Louisville, KY 40202-1396
Phone: (502) 569-5300

Organization: MV/USA is a program of the Presbyterian Church (USA) which helps church-related organizations to find full-time volunteers. To accomplish this, information is circulated on opportunities available, volunteers are recruited, orientation and other support services are provided, as is preliminary screening.

Program: MV placements may be in the U.S. or abroad; each year the organization places over 300 volunteers in positions in this country and over 100 overseas. The opportunities in the U.S. involve providing support services for educational institutions, serving in youth-related programs of congregations and childcare institutions, working in community service or special Christian education programs, camping and health care. There are summer service opportunities for 8 to 10 weeks and longer terms of one to two years. International assignments usually involve teaching (especially teaching English) and health care, with a few opportunities available each year for young adults in ecumenical programs in Europe.
Requirements: Skills required vary with assignment. Medical volunteers are usually doctors or nurses, but at times, paramedical personnel are needed as well. For international assignments, workers must be college graduates and have certification in TESOL or a teaching certificate. Spanish is helpful in some of the U.S. programs. For European placement, German or French may be required. All volunteers must be Christian and members of a church, though not necessarily Presbyterian.
Age: College age minimum; no maximum.
Living Arrangements: Vary with assignment.
Persons with Disabilities: Anyone may apply to volunteer. The only limitations are in the physical requirements of a particular project.
Finances: In general, room, board, and insurance coverage are provided for volunteers. Long-term volunteers may also receive a stipend for personal expenses.
Deadline: June 15 for appointments beginning the following January; December 15 for appointments beginning the following June.
Contact: Linda Crawford Hodges.

"My world view has been expanded dramatically. I am less rigid in terms of my views of other people and situations, as well as my own behavior. My faith was deepened by contact with Christians in such a difficult role."

National Farm Worker Ministry

1337 West Ohio, Room 310
Chicago, IL
60622
Phone: (312) 829-6436

Organization: The purpose of this ecumenical agency with 44 denominational and religious community members is "to support farm workers who are struggling for justice and self-determination."
Program: Volunteers serve for a minimum of one full year in California, Florida, Illinois, Michigan, New York, Ohio, or Texas. They organize support for the farm workers among the urban churches and work in farm worker organizing groups.
Requirements: Volunteers must be flexible, willing to work hard, and "committed to advocacy for justice." Spanish is helpful but not necessary.
Age: Minimum 18.
Living Arrangements: Volunteers

live in apartments or in communal houses.
Finances: Room and board are provided.
Deadline: None.
Contact: Sr. Patricia Drydyk, Executive Director.

The Ockenden Venture

Guildford Road
Woking, Surrey GU22 7UU,
England
Phone: (44-483) 772012

Organization: The Ockenden Venture is a registered British charity providing home, health, education, and rehabilitation for refugees in the United Kingdom and overseas. The United Kingdom bases include four reception centers for refugees and a home for physically and mentally handicapped young refugees.
Program: Volunteers are required to serve for at least one year at one of the U.K. centers. Training is provided and the volunteer may teach, undertake domestic duties, drive, carry out house maintenance, etc. They work with a small permanent staff gaining skills and insights into the needs and methods of working with the disadvantaged.
Requirements: There are no particular skills required.
Age: Minimum 18.
Living Arrangements: Accommodations are provided at the center where the volunteer is based.
Persons with Disabilities: Because of the nature of the work and the work site, there is little prospect of accepting volunteers with disabilities.

Finances: A weekly allowance of £22 is provided, plus room and board. Volunteers are required to make their own travel arrangements.
Deadline: Early application is recommended. August/September are our main months of entry but vacancies do occur at other times.
Contact: Personnel Officer.

Open Door Community

910 Ponce de Leon Avenue NE
Atlanta, GA 30306
Phone: (404) 874-9652

Organization: This is a residential Christian community that serves the homeless and prisoners in the Atlanta area. "First, we are servants to those in prison, especially those under the sentence of death. In the name of Jesus, we visit our condemned friends and witness against the death penalty in this state. Secondly, we serve the homeless and hungry on the streets of Atlanta. We share bread and beds with the poor and join our voices with the cries of the poor for justice in this city."
Program: Volunteers work in the Open Door soup kitchen or in the shelter, serve as shower supervisors, do advocacy for the homeless, visit prisoners, work with the families of prisoners and do some childcare when needed. "In all our work, we are called to practice hospitality and friendliness." Resident volunteers are asked for a minimum commitment of six months. Each volunteer is assigned to a "pastoral friend" who acts as a guide for the six-month term.
Requirements: There are no specific

skills required, just "a readiness to work with people."
Age: Minimum 25.
Living Arrangements: Volunteers have private accommodations within the 65-room shelter.
Finances: Room and board are provided, and there's a stipend of $50 per month. Even if the volunteer has other resources, he or she is asked to live on the room, board, and stipend.
Deadline: None.
Contact: Pat Fonz.

Overseas Development Network

333 Valencia Street, Suite 330
San Francisco, CA 94103
Phone: (415) 550-7069

Organization: ODN is an international student-based organization committed to educating students about global poverty, hunger, and injustice. Believing that education and action are inseparable, ODN promotes responsible involvement of its members in addressing the problems and potential solutions of global development. ODN connects students with community-based development projects around the world and creates a dynamic network of people striving for global grassroots development.
Program: ODN's office internship and fellowship programs give individuals an opportunity to become involved in global development issues, nonprofit management, and student organizaing. Interns are assigned to a specific project based on the needs of the office as well as the intern's experience, skills, and interests. Examples of projects include development education coordination, publications research, conference organizing, membership development, and fundraising.
Requirements: Interns should be willing and able to serve as a member of a team, in a cooperative effort to integrate the ideas of all involved. Oral and written comunication skills are important and an ability to use MacIntosh computers is very helpful. Most essential is an interest or experience in student activism and organizing and the desire to learn more and educate others about issues related to international solidarity and Third World development.
Age: Persons of all ages and backgrounds are encouraged to apply.
Living Arrangements: ODN does not provide housing for volunteers.
Finances: Due to ODN's limited budget, most internships are unpaid. Work-study funds are available to eligible students. ODN also encourages students of color to apply for its Office Fellowship Program which offers fellows a small stipend.
Deadline: None.

Partnership for Service Learning

815 Second Avenue
Suite 315
New York, NY 10017
Phone: (212) 986-0989

Organization: The Partnership is a consortium of colleges, universities, and service agencies organized na-

tionally and internationally, which provides opportunities for students to combine their formal studies with an international/intercultural experience through community service.
Program: Semester, year, summer, and January intersession programs are available in Ecuador, England and Scotland, France, India, Jamaica, Liberia, Mexico, the Philippines, and South Dakota. The programs combine academic study with community service. The studies are given through accredited colleges in the host country; academic credit is granted from the student's home college. Service opportunities vary, but generally involve human services, teaching, health care, special education, English as a second language, and community development. The service takes place 20 to 35 hours a week. Undergraduates, recent graduates, professionals, and high school seniors are invited to apply.
Requirements: "Motivation to be of meaningful service is more important than special skills."
Age: Minimum 18.
Living Arangements: Student participants usually live with families, at the host college, or in the service agency.
Finances: A fee which covers orientation, instruction, room, board, and related costs is charged. Participants make their own arrangements for transportation to and from workcamps and spending money. Financial aid can apply for registered students. Program costs range from $1,400 to $3,400.
Deadline: Two months before the start of the program.

Contact: Howard A. Berry, Linda A. Chisolm, Co-Directors.

"I found that I couldn't change the world, but I did teach four children to read."

Peace Corps

1990 K Street NW
Washington, DC 20526
Phone: (202) 606-3387

Organization: Since the Peace Corps was established by President John F. Kennedy in 1961, over 131,000 Americans have served. Volunteers work on projects determined by the communities themselves.
Program: An 8- to 12-week training period precedes the two-year Peace Corps assignment; during training, volunteers study the culture and the language of the people they'll be living with. Some sample Peace Corps volunteer projects: a volunteer in Tonga assisted a public health project physician; one helped develop disease-resistant vegetables in Western Samoa; another trained teachers and developed a library in Nepal.
Requirements: The Peace Corps is looking for volunteers with practical experience. All volunteers must be U.S. citizens. Specialists are needed in the areas of agriculture, architecture, business, engineering, forestry, fishing, health, home economics, math and sciences, skilled trades such as masonry and plumbing, and teaching. Under a category they call "generalists," the Peace Corps recruits volunteers with degrees in social work and liberal arts or with

experience in handicrafts, home management, and various trades. A knowledge of the host country's language is helpful, but not required. "If you can talk to people, give them confidence, and help them find resources and make the best use of them, you're needed. If you're persevering and adaptable, creative in problem solving, anxious to learn from others, the odds are you're a good candidate for the Peace Corps."
Age: Minimum 18.
Living Arrangements: Accommodations are provided in the host community.
Persons with Disabilities: Applications are welcomed from persons with disabilities.
Finances: Volunteers receive a living allowance that is enough to cover housing, food, and the essentials with a little left over for spending money. When the voluntary service assignment is complete, volunteers receive a readjustment allowance of $200 for every month served.
Deadline: Applications should be received at least six to nine months but no more than one year before you expect to be available for assignment.
Contact: Office of Volunteer Recruitment and Service.

Peace Village International

Pfeilstrasse 35
D-4200 Oberhausen 14
Germany

Organization: The organization is involved in medical treatment for children from crisis areas and operates a peace education school.
Program: Volunteers are needed for social service projects. The minimum period of service is three months.
Requirements: Volunteers should be able to speak German.
Age: Minimum 18.
Living Arrangements: Volunteers live in shared accommodations.
Persons with Disabilities: Applications are assessed on an individual basis.
Finances: Room and board are provided.
Deadline: None.

Ponape Agriculture and Trade School

P.O. Box 39
Pohnpei, Caroline Islands, FM 96941
Phone: (691) 320-2991

Organization: This is an agriculture and trade school in Micronesia which is staffed by volunteers, members of the Jesuit order, and Micronesians, most of whom are PATS graduates.
Program: PATS is a four-year vocational school. Students specialize in agriculture, mechanics, or construction. Volunteers serve at PATS for two years starting in mid-July. They teach English (the native language is Ponopean), math, science, agriculture, architecture, mechanics, and construction.
Requirements: U.S. volunteers must be college graduates or have skilled experience in a trade taught at PATS.
Age: No set minimum or maximum.
Living Arrangements: Men live in a dormitory with private rooms; women share a small three-bedroom

house located on campus. PATS is located in a rather isolated spot; mail is delivered two to three times a week from Kolonia, the capital of Ponape, which is one hour's drive away on a coral road.

Persons with Disabilities: If the applicant can handle the rural environment and has the ability to walk great distances they will be considered.

Finances: Room and board and round-trip plane fare are provided plus a small monthly stipend.

Deadline: March 1 (flexible).

Contact: Rev. Joseph A. Cavanagh, Director.

"The interaction and unselfish giving that takes place between the volunteer and the student and the volunteer and his coworkers, is the action side of the PATS spiritual life."

Project Concern International/Options Service

P.O. Box 85323
San Diego, CA 92186
Phone: (619) 279-9690

Organization: This is a nonprofit personnel agency which places health care and development specialists in rural areas of Africa, Asia, Eastern Europe, and North and South America. The agency's parent foundation is Project Concern.

Program: Volunteers may serve from three months to two years. They are all medical and health professionals who choose the positions that interest them from a regularly compiled list of openings. Some of the positions are more like jobs than voluntary service, but others fit into the latter category. Some examples of recent openings: a surgeon in Kenya to be in charge of a 120-bed hospital, registered nurses in Uganda to teach in a hospital, a doctor or nurse with childcare experience to work in an orphanage in rural India, ophthalmologists to do cataract surgery in primitive conditions in Nepal, etc.

Requirements: All applicants must be licensed in their field.

Age: Minimum 18.

Living Arrangements: Vary with assignment. Room and board are almost always provided; some positions also have salaries, stipends, travel funds, etc. Options charges a $10 annual fee for its services.

Persons with Disabilities: Options refers individuals to facilities; thus, the policy depends on the facility. Options will, however, refer anyone qualified for any position, regardless of their disability status.

Finances: Arrangements vary according to placement.

Deadline: None.

Contact: Placement Director, Options Department.

Project HOPE

Millwood, VA 22646
Phone: (703) 837-2100

Organization: The Project began with the S.S. Hope, the world's first peacetime hospital ship. More than 33 years later, Project HOPE continues to provide health manpower training and education programs in developing nations with the goal of helping

the people of those nations assume full responsibility for education and treatment programs. Since its founding, over 4,000 HOPE educators have trained thousands of health care personnel.
Program: Volunteers—physicians, nurses, and allied health personnel—serve short-term (less than six months) or long-term (at least one year) at program sites all over the world.
Requirements: Certification in professional area and at least two full years of recent work experience in their specialty area. Other requirements depend on individual assignments.
Finances: Short-term volunteers receive transportation, housing, and a per diem; long-term volunteers receive transportation, salary, and a relocation allowance.
Deadline: None.
Contact: International Recruitment Section.

Queen Louise Home for Children

Lutheran Social Services of the U.S. Virgin Islands
Box 866 Frederiksted
St. Croix U.S.V.I. 00841
Phone: (809) 772-0090

Organization: Lutheran Social Services is the official agency of the Caribbean Synod of the Evangelical Lutheran Church in America. The organization owns and operates the Queen Louise Home for Children, a residential child care facility in the U.S. Virgin Islands. The program provides temporary care for abused, abandoned, neglected, and developmentally disabled children.
Program: Volunteers serve from a year to 18 months. Volunteers care for groups of approximately 10 children between the ages of 3 and 12 and also maintain the living areas.
Requirements: A college degree is preferred and knowledge of Spanish is helpful.
Age: Most volunteers are between the ages of 25 and 45.
Living Arrangements: Room and board are provided for volunteers in small apartments.
Persons with Disabilities: Positions for persons with disabilities can be discussed on an individual basis.
Finances: A biweekly stipend of $103 is provided. Medical insurance is provided.
Deadline: None.
Contact: Masserae Sprauve, Director.

Richmond Fellowship International

8 Addison Road
Kensington, London W14 8DL
England
Phone: (44-71) 603-6373/6374

Organization: Richmond Fellowship International is a charity based in the U.K. with connections in Australia, Austria, Canada, Hong Kong, India, Israel, Mexico, New Zealand, Peru, Uruguay, the U.S., and the Caribbean. It provides therapeutic communities for adults and adolescents with mental health problems. One of the main

tasks is to help people take their place in society after a breakdown.
Program: Volunteers are mainly placed in the U.K. and the U.S.; there may occasionally be opportunities in other countries. The minimum commitment is for six months in the U.K. and one year in the U.S.
Requirements: Volunteers should be mature and stable, with understanding, tolerance, and intelligence, and the ability to form good relationships with others. Skills required are a good knowledge of English, teaching experience, social work, or nursing qualification. Training in music, handicraft, office administration and an interest in homemaking, cooking, and gardening are relevant.
Age: Minimum 21.
Living Arrangements: Volunteers live in separate rooms if available.
Finances: Room and board are provided as well as a stipend of £25 per week in the U.K. and $40 in the U.S. In the U.S., this increases to $60 per week after six months.
Deadline: None.
Contact: Dr. Edith Waldman, Executive Officer; include a brief curriculum vitae with the initial letter. An interview, usually in London, will be required. Interview expenses cannot be refunded.

St. Joseph's Indian School

Box 89
Chamberlain, SD 57325
Phone: (605) 734-6021

Organization: St. Joseph's is a Catholic boarding school established 60 years ago to provide for the spiritual, educational, emotional, and physical welfare of Native American children in need.
Program: Volunteers serve for one year, usually beginning in August at the start of the school term. They may act as houseparents, teachers or infirmary personnel (nurses or aides). The school is located in Chamberlain (population 2,258), a town on the banks of the Missouri River. Volunteers arrive in mid-August for a two-week orientation to the school, the area and the background of Native Americans.
Requirements: Houseparents should have a experience working with children, teachers need a teaching degree and should be certifiable in South Dakota. Nurses must be registered or have an LPN. "Fair, consistent, patient and active are good adjectives to describe desirable staff members."
Age: Minimum 21.
Finances: Room and board, health and life insurance, and a salary are provided for houseparents; teachers receive a salary, insurance, and retirement benefits.
Deadline: None.
Contact: Kim Tyrell, Personnel.

Shaftesbury Society

Holiday Centre
New Hall, Low Road
Dovercourt, Harwich, Essex C012 3TS
England
Phone: (44-255) 504219

Organization: The Society is a Christian charity which cares for physically handicapped children and adults in

schools, hostels, and mission and holiday centers.
Program: The Society operates a holiday center in Dovercourt, Essex, where each year hundreds of disabled and elderly men and women enjoy a vacation by the sea. Volunteers are recruited to help these people get the most from their holiday; they escort guests to shops or to the beach or outings. They help guests dress, eat, etc. Duties may also include bed making, laundry, dining-room duty, and a number of other miscellaneous tasks. Volunteers serve for one to four weeks between April and October.
Requirements: Qualified nurses are useful, but volunteers are not required to be experienced as long as they are willing and able to care for the handicapped guests according to their needs. "As a Christian organization, we require our volunteers to be at least sympathetic to our Christian position."
Age: 16–70.
Living Arrangements: Volunteers live at the center and may be asked to share a bedroom with another volunteer.
Finances: Room and board are provided as well as transportation by bus between London and Dovercourt.
Deadline: None.
Contact: Pat Ford.

"The unity of the team and the love of each member for others and the Lord, spoke more profoundly to me than a thousand sermons."

Sherut La'am

American Zionist Youth Foundation
515 Park Avenue
New York, NY 10022
Phone: (212) 751-6070

Organization: AZYF strives to "instill in young Jews a strong sense of Jewish identity and a deep devotion to the land of Israel."
Program: Sherut La'am, which means "service to the people" in Hebrew, is the voluntary service program of AZYF. There are actually two Sherut La'am programs: one for six months, the other for one year. The one-year program begins in August; the six-month program may begin at any time. Volunteers live and work in development towns. They may be involved in health care, social work, science, computers, architecture; physical, occupational or speech therapy; environmental protection; or teaching. AZYF staff tries to match the skills and interests of applicants with the jobs to be done. Usually, people with backgrounds in liberal arts or social sciences are placed in jobs in the educational system or in community centers. The one-year program includes three months of Hebrew study (the Ulpan) and nine months of work.
Requirements: Applicants to the one-year program must be between the ages of 20 and 35 and hold a degree from a four-year college or university or a two-year technical/vocational institute. Married couples without children are eligible. Participants in the six-month program must have completed at least one year of college

or vocational training, and must have a good conversational knowledge of Hebrew. Volunteers with a liberal arts degree usually teach English. "We have found that the following characteristics seem to facilitate social and vocational integration and adjustment: independence, creativity, initiative, flexibility, and a sense of humor."
Age: 20–35.
Living Arrangements: Three or four volunteers share an apartment.
Persons with Disabilities: It is difficult to place persons with disabilities.
Finances: Participants pay their own airfare. The one-year program costs $1,000; the six-month program costs $750. Housing and a monthly stipend for food are provided.
Deadline: Two months before departure.
Contact: Julie Pavlovsky, Long Term Programs.

"Looking back on my ten months as a Sherut La'am volunteer, I feel that I have accomplished almost everything I set out to do...I am leaving with strong feelings for the country."

Simon Community

P.O. Box 1187
London NW5 4HW
England
Phone: (44-71) 485-6639

Organization: Founded in 1963, the Simon Community serves the homeless and rootless people of London—the people who have been rejected by society and who, without support of family and friends, "have slipped through the net of the welfare state." The Community operates night shelters and houses of hospitality. It has no paid staff ("We try to break down the division between helping and being helped"), receives no government funding and tries to develop the Community along democratic lines. Simon is "Catholic-founded and inspired but is completely ecumenical with members of all faiths and none. Without preaching or tracts, it aims to put into practice the single gospel message."
Program: Everyone who works at the Simon Community is a volunteer. They come from a variety of backgrounds, are at different stages in their lives, and serve for a minimum of three months. "Their role can be crucial, not to dominate but to provide support and a sympathetic ear and instill a sense of direction into the community providing an example by the quality of their caring." A typical day includes domestic chores, spending time with residents in order to gain their trust and possibly provide support, and outreach work.
Requirements: There are no specific qualifications except patience, tolerance, stamina, and a good sense of humor.
Age: Minimum 20.
Living Arrangements: Simon workers live with residents in basic conditions, sharing their food and facilities. Workers have one free day each week.
Finances: Full board and a small weekly stipend are provided. There's a 10-day leave every three months with leave allowance.
Deadline: None.
Contact: Community Leaders.

SMA Lay Missionaries

256 N. Manor Circle
Takoma Park, MD 20912
Phone: (301) 891-2037

Organization: The Society of African Missions is an international Catholic missionary community specializing in missionary work with Africans and people of African descent. The SMA lay mission program is a practical way by which Catholic laity who feel called to African missionary service can fit into an already established and well-experienced instrument of evangelization.
Program: The SMA Lay Missionaries seek candidates who are willing to serve for at least two years in Africa. Lay Missionaries are sought from the fields of pastoral care, teaching, health care, building, agriculture, and business. Missions are in West Africa.
Requirements: Applicants must be practicing Catholics with a college degree, two years work experience, "mature faith commitment, strong missionary desire, and usable skills for mission work." Candidates undergo a process of screening and discernment before entering into missionary formation in Takoma Park, Maryland. Lay men and women, married or single (but without dependents) are eligible to apply.
Age: 23–50.
Living Arrangements: SMA Lay Missionaries live in SMA communities on the mission.
Persons with Disabilities: All applications are considered on an individual basis.
Finances: SMA Lay Missionaries receive a monthly stipend, room and board, and transportation to and from the mission site.
Deadline: April 1 for September formation program.
Contact: Rev. Douglas Gilbert, Director.

Stella Maris School of Nursing

Apartado Postal 28
Zacapu, Michoacan, Mexico 58680
Phone: (52-456) 313-00

Organization: Stella Maris is a three-year school of nursing with over 200 students. The school was founded in 1967 by Sister Theresa Avila, a nurse and Catholic nun from California who remains the chief administrator. The school prepares quality nurses who can improve health care in the towns and pueblos of the region which is between Mexico City and Guadalajara. "Our students usually come from poor families, and we strive to make their education as inexpensive as possible."
Program: Volunteers serve for six months or more as community health assistants, clinical supervisors, nursing teachers, secretaries, librarians, and handymen. "We need help now more than ever with the economy in Mexico the way it is."
Requirements: Teachers should be nurses, doctors, or chemists, but for some positions, no special skills are required. Teachers must be fluent in Spanish; others should be able to at least communicate in the language.
Age: 21–60.

Living Arrangements: Volunteers live in a large 12-room house. Meals are provided at the house, and volunteers eat together family-style.
Persons with Disabilities: Depending on the nature of the disability, persons with disabilities are accepted.
Finances: Room, board, and a small monthly stipend are provided.
Deadline: None.
Contact: Volunteer Coordinator. (Send a resume and photo with your request for an application.)

Tallahatchie Development League

P.O. Box 267
Tutwiler, MS 38963
Phone: (601) 345-8574

Organization: The League promotes community development in the areas of economics, education, and family life, and serves as a liaison between people and resources.
Program: Volunteers may participate in short-term or long-term projects that involve construction, teaching, Bible study, office work, or nutrition. Most volunteers come in preformed groups. Some projects that the League sponsors include meals on wheels, youth recreation, counseling, housing development programs, and a legal counseling program for people who need help in the area of domestic relations.
Requirements: Skills must match the placement.
Age: Minimum age is 14 for groups as long as there's an adult adviser.
Living Arrangements: Groups stay in individual rooms in private homes.
Persons with Disabilities: Persons with disabilities are encouraged to apply.
Finances: Groups pay for their own food and some supplies.
Deadline: None.
Contact: Larry Haynes, Executive Director.

United Church Board for Homeland Ministries

700 Prospect Avenue
Cleveland, OH 44115-1100
Phone: (216) 736-3262

Organization: UCBHM acts as a clearinghouse for voluntary service opportunities all over the U.S. Some of the community organizations listed in *Volunteer!* use the Board to help with recruitment.
Program: UCBHM administers both a one-year and a short-term voluntary service program as well as summer service opportunities. The one-year program may involve a placement in a youth home, a home for the aged, a program for the retarded, a community organizing effort, a hunger or peace action project and others. Summer opportunities involve a one- to three-month commitment to an institution, a community, or a camp.
Requirements: Some positions require no special skills, others require professional degrees. A religious affiliation is not required, but participants "must respect our religious basis for service."
Age: Minimum 18.
Living Arrangements: These vary

from project to project; some involve living in a residential institution, others offer accommodations in an apartment or a private home.

Persons with Disabilities: Persons with disabilities are accepted into the program depending on the organization's ability to place them in a position which can use their skills and provide facilities for them. UCBHM "seeks placement opportunities for persons who are differently abled."

Finances: One-year volunteers receive room and board, a small monthly stipend, some insurance coverage, and transportation home after service. Short-term volunteers pay a program fee and their own transportation to and from the project site. Room and board are provided during the term of service.

Deadline: None for long-term program; placement usually takes about two months. May 1 is the deadline for summer placement applications.

Contact: Susan M. Sanders, Secretary for Voluntary Service.

United Methodist Volunteers In Mission

Southern Jurisdiction
159 Ralph McGill Boulevard, NE
Room 305
Atlanta, GA 30308
Phone: (404) 659-5060

Organization: This United Methodist organization matches individuals and groups to mission projects in the U.S. and abroad. It provides coordination, placement, training, insurance, and debriefing.

Program: A wide range of long- and short-term opportunities in almost any field of community service are

A United Methodist Volunteer makes paper toys with children in Mérida, Mexico.

offered including building, counseling, children's services, office assistance in church programs, and teaching. Opportunities are primarily in the Americas and the Caribbean, but also in Africa, Europe, and Asia.

Requirements: Some training or experience in a practical field is usually essential. Bilingualism is encouraged. Volunteers need not be church members but all must adhere to the moral standard of the host community.

Age: Minimum 18.

Living Arrangements: The host country provides housing.

Persons with Disabilities: Persons with disabilities are welcome.

Finances: There is a nonreturnable administration fee of $25 for domestic appicants and $50 for international applicants, to accompany the application form. Room and board is available for some placements.

Deadline: Three months in advance of desired service period. Only residents of Alabama, Florida, Georgia, Kentucky, Missippi, North Carolina, South Carolina, Tennessee, and Virginia should apply to this office. Others should contact the United Methodist Church in their area.

Contact: Director.

United Nations Volunteer Program

Palais des Nations
1211 Geneva 10
Switzerland
Phone: (41-22) 788-2455

Organization: In 1970, the Secretary-General of the United Nations recommended the establishment of a volunteer scheme that would operate within the United Nations system. UNV's main activity is to program, deliver, and administer suitably qualified, experienced, and motivated personnel for international technical cooperation with developing countries.

Program: Over 2,000 UN volunteer specialists and grassroots field workers of more than 100 nationalities are currently assigned to over 100 countries, in projects executed by organizations of the UN system such as FAO, ILO, UNDP, UNESCO, UNHCR, UNICEF, WFP, and WHO, or by developing country governments or UNV itself.

Requirements: First and/or postgraduate degree, or equivalent technical qualifications. Minimum two, preferably several years working experience. Contracts usually run two years, with exceptions in the context of emergency programs.

Age: Minimum 21; no maximum. The current average age is 38.

Living Arrangements: The host country provides housing.

Finances: Volunteers receive a monthly living allowance, currently between $600 and $1,200 a month depending on the local cost of living; sickness and accident insurance; return airfare; and a modest resettlement allowance.

Deadline: None.

United States Forest Service—Alaska Region

P.O. Box 21628
Juneau, AK 99802-1628
Phone: (907) 586-8801

Organization: The Alaska Region of the U.S. Forest Service is responsible for the nation's two largest national forests: the Tongass National Forest (17 million acres) in southeastern Alaska and the Chugach National Forest (6 million acres) in southern Alaska.

Program: Volunteer positions available in the Alaska Region include but are not limited to: interpreters, archaeology aides, fishery aides, wildlife habitat maintenance and protection aides, forestry aides, trail maintenance assistants, wilderness rangers, campground hosts, cooks, survey crew members, maintenance workers, clerical assistants, warehouse assistants, and information aides. Both short- and long-term opportunities are available. Volunteers may work full- or part-time.

Requirements: None, but those with skills are more easily placed.

Age: Minimum 16.

Living Arrangements: Accommodations vary from crew quarters at field locations to in-town apartments.

Persons with Disabilities: Persons with disabilities are welcomed.

Finances: Volunteers generally receive housing and a daily allowance of $23 for food. In some cases, housing is not provided.

Deadline: None.

Contact: Regional Volunteer Coordinator.

United States Forest Service—Northern Region

Federal Building
P.O. Box 7669
Missoula, MT 59807

Organization: The Northern Region of the U.S. Forest Service is responsible for federal lands in Montana, northern Idaho, western North Dakota, and part of northwest South Dakota.

Program: Volunteers are needed to work on conservation projects, campground hosting, wildlife management, and assisting with teaching and counseling in job corps centers. Opportunities can last from one day to years but are mainly available from may to October.

Requirements: None.

Age: No age limits; those under 16 require parental approval.

Living Arrangements: Some projects provide food and house volunteers in bunk houses, rental units, or tents.

Persons with Disabilities: Depending on the tasks, persons with disabilities are welcome to apply.

Finances: Room and board are sometimes provided.

Deadline: Open year-round; for spring and summer openings, applications are needed by April.

Contact: Human Resource Programs.

United States Forest Service—Pacific Northwest Region

P.O. Box 3623
Portland, OR 97208
Phone: (503) 326-3816

Organization: The Pacific Northwest Region of the U.S. Forest Service maintains 19 national forests in Oregon and Washington.
Program: Volunteers are needed to maintain trails, campgrounds, wildlife, and timber.
Requirements: The organization tries to tailor jobs to match vounteers' skills.
Living Arrangements: Vary, but may be a bunkhouse, cabin, or shared housing of some other kind.
Persons with Disabilities: The organization works to find ways to accommodate individual needs.
Finances: Full-time volunteers usually receive room and board; living allowances can be negotiated.
Deadline: None.
Contact: Volunteer Coordinator.

Vincentian Service Corps

St. John's University, SJH-116
Jamaica, NY 11439
Phone: (718) 990-6266

Organization: Founded in 1983, the VSC allows men and women to serve the urban poor.
Program: Volunteers perform community service in a variety of positions such as social work, teaching, childcare, and health care. Positions are predominantly in Northeastern urban settings. Volunteers serve for one year. Each volunteer meets with a supervisor on a weekly basis.
Requirements: Participants generally have a college degree or two years of work experience. Volunteers must be Christian.
Age: Minimum 20.
Living Arrangements: Volunteers live in community houses or apartments.
Persons with Disabilities: Volunteers must be able to function at the placement.
Finances: Room, board, medical insurance, and a monthly stipend are provided.
Deadline: None.
Contact: Bernard M. Tracey.

Visions in Action

3637 Fulton Street NW
Washington, DC 20007
Phone (202) 625-7403

Organization: Visions in Action is a nonprofit, nonsectarian organization offering one-year internships in African and Indian cities.
Program: Volunteers are stationed in India, Kenya, South Africa, Uganda, West Africa, and Zimbabwe. Positions are available with African nonprofit organizations, health clinics, magazines, newspapers, and research institutes. Duties may include conservation, construction, education, editing and writing, health services, management, research, or social services.
Requirements: Applicants must have completed their second year of college or have the equivalent ex-

perience. Most interns are recent college graduates or graduate students.
Age: None.
Living Arrangements: Interns live in urban areas, in group houses or with families in middle-income areas.
Persons with Disabilities: Persons with disabilities must be able to work in possibly adverse conditions.
Finances: Interns are expected to cover their own costs and encouraged to fundraise. Participants are insured.
Deadline: Varies with location.
Contact: Sutia Kim Alter, U.S. Director.

VISTA

1100 Vermont Avenue NW
Washington, DC 20525
Phone: (202) 606-4845

Organization: VISTA (Volunteers in Service to America) is a full-time volunteer program of ACTION, the U.S. government umbrella organization for voluntary service. VISTA recruits people of all ages and backgrounds who are committed to increasing the capability of low-income people to improve the conditions of their lives.
Program: Volunteers are assigned to local sponsors. They live and work among the poor, serving in urban and rural areas.
Requirements: VISTA needs people who have skill and experience in conducting education or literacy programs, in working with runaway youth or low-income seniors, or in helping with neighborhood revitalization and economic development.
Living Arrangements: Volunteers live in the communities they serve.
Finances: Volunteers receive a subsistence allowance covering housing, food, and incidentals as well as a $90 per month stipend paid when the term of service is completed.

Volunteers for Educational and Social Services

3001 South Congress
Austin, TX 78704
Phone: (512) 447-6144

Organization: VESS was founded in 1972 under the auspices of the Texas Catholic Conference. It helps staff Catholic schools, parishes, social service agencies, shelters, clinics, and other sites devoted to responding to the needy people of Texas. Those served come from a variety of religious and ethnic backgrounds.
Program: Positions in social work, teaching, nursing, religious education, youth ministry, halfway houses and others. Teachers serve 10 months, others one year. "VESS emphasizes the professional and personal development of all members."
Requirements: A bachelor's degree is preferred. Teachers must be college graduates. Nurses must pursue licensure once in Texas. Some positions require the ability to speak Spanish.
Age: Minimum 21.
Living Arrangements: Volunteers most often live with one another in shared houses or apartments; each person has his or her own bedroom.
Persons with Disabilities: VESS attempts to place persons with disabilities in suitable positions.

162 Volunteer!

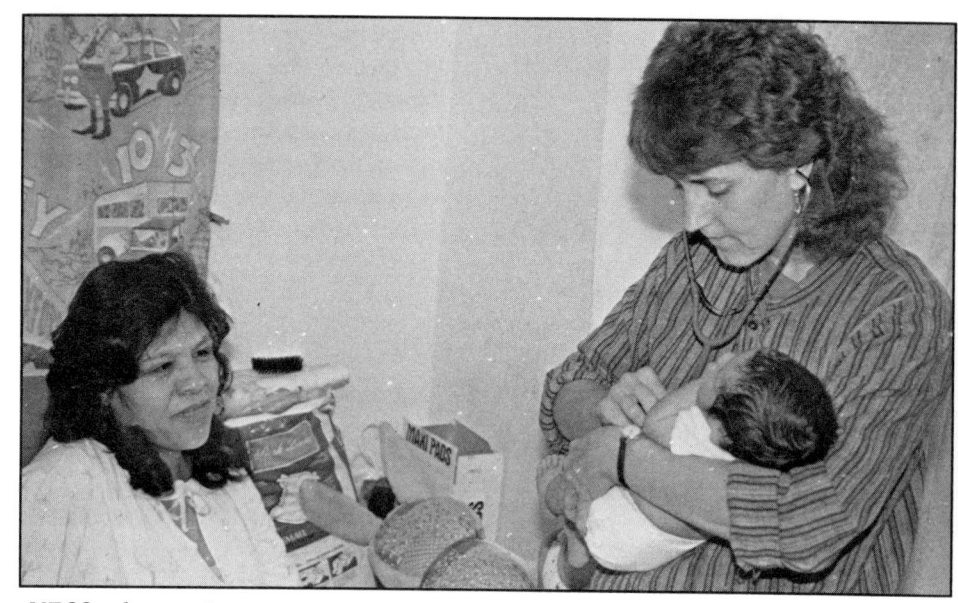

VESS volunteer Janet Berning working as a nurse at the Holy Family Services Birthing Center.

Finances: Room and board, a monthly stipend and food allowance, and insurance are provided. Orientation and in-service training are provided. Scholarships are possible for volunteers signing successive contracts.
Contact: Colleen Pritchard, Volunteer Development Coordinator.

Volunteers in Technical Assistance

1815 North Lynn Street, Suite 200
Arlington, VA 22209
Phone: (703) 276-1800

Organization: VITA is a private, non-profit organization which provides technical assistance to people in developing countries.
Program: Volunteer opportunities include responding to technical inquiries by mail and occasionally on-site consulting. Consultations on projects may last for several months.
Requirements: Technical and managerial skills are required of volunteers. Knowledge of a language other than English and three to five years of overseas work experience is highly desirable.
Finances: All expenses are paid by VITA for on-site consultations.
Contact: Brij Mathur, Director of Information Service.

World Assembly of Youth

Ved Bellahøj 4
DK-2700 Brønshøj
Copenhagen, Denmark
Phone: (45) 3160-7770

Organization: WAY is an international coordinating body of national youth organizations.

Program: WAY coordinates community service projects in all nations except Angola, Cambodia, Cuba, Ethiopia, North Korea, South Africa, and Vietnam. It needs volunteers to staff its headquarters in Copenhagen for periods of one year.
Requirements: Volunteers should have experience in development management and program development. French- and Spanish-speakers are preferred.
Age: Under 35.
Living Arrangements: Volunteers share a second-floor flat in Copenhagen.
Finances: Volunteers receive a monthly stipend of $500 for meals and other expenses. Volunteers are also insured.
Deadline: None.
Contact: Shiv Khare, Secretary-General.

World Council of Churches

Sub-Unit on Youth
P.O. Box 2100
150, Route de Ferney
1211 Geneva 2, Switzerland

Organization: World Council of Churches recruits young people to serve in underdeveloped countries.
Program: Each summer, several workcamps are organized in Africa, Asia, and the Middle East for two to four weeks. Volunteers are involved in activities such as building roads, agricultural work, renovation of buildings, and other manual work.
Requirements: None.
Age: 18–30.
Living Arrangements: Vary.

Finances: Volunteers pay their own travel expenses. They are expected to make a contribution of approximately $10 per day for general living expenses of the camp.
Deadline: None.

WorldTeach

Harvard Institute for International Development
One Eliot Street
Cambridge, MA 02138-5705
Phone: (617) 495-5527

Organization: WorldTeach is a non-profit program of Harvard University's social service organization, the Phillips Brooks House Association.
Program: Volunteers are needed to spend one year teaching at schools in Costa Rica, Namibia, Poland, and Thailand, as well as to instruct athletics in South Africa and English in Shanghai for shorter periods.
Requirements: A bachelor's degree is required for year-long programs, and some experience in sports coaching or participation is necessary for the coaching program in South Africa.
Age: Many volunteers are recent college graduates, but WorldTeach encourages retired and mid-career applicants as well. The Shanghai Summer Teaching Program volunteers are undergraduate and active graduate students.
Living Arrangements: Volunteers stay in housing provided by the school.
Finances: The fee for participation is $3,150 to $4,360. Housing and a modest salary are provided.

164 Volunteer!

WorldTeach sports instructors celebrate with soccer players in Khayelitsha, Cape Town, South Africa.

Deadline: Four to six months prior to departure.

"I like looking into all the faces and eyes and seeing the ones that are really shining, whether it is out of interest and understanding or something else. This is what keeps me going, even on bad days."

World Vision

919 West Huntington Drive
Monrovia, CA 91016
Phone: (818) 357-7979

Organization: World Vision was founded in 1950. It is an international Christian humanitarian agency working in more than 90 nations.
Program: World Vision hires expatriates when technical expertise cannot be found within developing countries. Only experts in their field can be considered for overseas assignments. Full-time expatriate needs usually include proficiency in public health, agriculture, financial management, accounting, logistics, or commodities.
Requirements: Volunteers must have no less than two years of previous Third World experience in their field of expertise. They must be fluent in a language appropriate to the country of placement. They must possess a strong Christian commitment that complements World Vision's own evangelical mandate.
Living Arrangements: Accommodations are usually quite primitive.
Finances: World Vision supplies contract workers with airfare to and from the assigned field project, room and board, a monthly stipend, and health insurance.
Contact: Employment.

The WUJS Institute

American Zionist Youth Foundation (AZYF)
110 East 59th Street
New York, NY 10022
Phone: (212) 339-6933

Organization: The WUJS Institute offers young professionals from all over the world the opportunity to spend one year in Israel studying Hebrew and Judaism while practicing their professions.
Program: The Institute, located in the town of Arad on the Dead Sea, offers beginning to advanced Hebrew courses. After five and a half months of language instruction and Jewish/Israeli studies, graduates disperse across the country to work in their professional fields. The WUJS Opportunities in Israel Department assists students in finding salaried work and to explore other options, such as working on a kibbutz, continued university studies, volunteer internships, military service, and studying in a Yeshiva.
Requirements: Applicants must have a four-year college degree or similar qualifications. Married couples without children are also eligible. Participants must commit to spending one full year in Israel from the commencement of their session.
Age: 21–35.
Living Arrangements: Students live in furnished apartments, sometimes sharing bedrooms. Individual apartments are available for married participants. The Institute has its own language lab, library, synagogue, student lounge, and laundromat, and is located across the street from the main shopping center of Arad. "The people of Arad welcome WUJS students into their community and into their homes."
Finances: Room and a daily main meal are provided by the Institute. Students receive a monthly stipend towards expenses for breakfast and supper. The fee for tourists is $1,400 plus $150 for medical insurance. A refundable deposit of $100 is also required.
Deadline: Program starting dates are January 7, April 28, July 28, and October 27.
Contact: Julie Pavlovsky, Long Term Programs.

Wycliffe Bible Translators

Box 2727
Huntington Beach, CA 92647
Phone: (714) 969-4600

Organization: This Christian organization focuses on linguistics research, Bible translation, literacy, and intercultural community work. "We believe that to accomplish Christ's commission, the Gospel must be presented to everyone in the language he understands best. Every person needs at least some of the written Scriptures in his mother tongue."
Program: The program is carried on largely by career members who are supported by churches, other organizations, and interested individuals. Volunteers who serve for one to two years (these are called short-term assistants) are invited to fill specific needs of field offices in over 50 different countries. Half of the

staff is involved in translation and literacy work, the other half serves as pilots, teachers, secretaries, doctors, accountants, buyers, shippers, nurses, radio operators, artists, builders, etc.
Requirements: These vary with the assignment.
Age: Minimum 21.
Living Arrangements: These vary enormously—from privately-owned to organizationally-owned to rented housing.
Persons with Disabilities: Applications by volunteers with disabilities are handled on a case by case basis.
Finances: Volunteers must pay their own travel expenses and support themselves while on assignment. Most get financial help from churches and/or interested individuals and friends.
Deadline: None.
Contact: Wayne Aeschliman, Director of Personnel, U.S. Division.

YMCA of the USA

International Office for Asia
909 Fourth Avenue
Seattle, WA 98104
Phone: (206) 382-5008

Organization: The YMCA's International Office for Asia assists YMCAs in Japan and Taiwan by recruiting people to teach conversational English in community-based YMCAs throughout those countries.
Program: Volunteers teach English as a second language in YMCAs throughout Japan and Taiwan. Students range in age from 5 to 70 years old. Volunteers teach for a minimum of two years in Japan (beginning either April 1 or September 1), and for a minimum of one year in Taiwan (beginning July 1 or October 1).
Requirements: Volunteers must have a B.A. Teaching experience is helpful, as is some knowledge of Japanese, Mandarin, or Taiwanese.
Age: College graduate.
Living Arrangements: In Japan, an apartment is provided; in Taiwan, either an apartment or a homestay.
Persons with Disabilities: As volunteers are employees of YMCAs in Japan and Taiwan, they need to be able to live self-sufficiently in either country.
Finances: A $25 fee is charged for administrative costs. In Japan, salaries begin at ¥210,000 a month and increase depending on educational and professional background. In addition, insurance, round-trip airfare, and 30 paid vacation days are provided. In Taiwan, volunteers are paid NT$12,000 for the first six months and NT$14,400 for the second six months. In addition, insurance, return airfare, round-trip airfare to Hong Kong, and a week's paid vacation (after the first six months) are provided.
Deadline: For Japan, October 5 (for April) and March 15 (for September). For Taiwan, January 15 (for July) and April 15 (for October).
Contact: Bonnie Main, OSCY Program Administrator.

"This has been a cultural jolt to me, yet each day is experienced as a new adventure. I occasionally look back at my years in the corporate environment and it seems as if I were another person."

APPENDIX

Appendix I
Council of Religious Volunteer Agencies (CRVA)

The members of the Council of Religious Volunteer Agencies are:

Chris Bekemeier
  Lutheran Volunteer Corps

Bill Berry
  Baptist Home Mission Board

Sr. Ellen Cavanaugh
  International Liaison

Tom Curtis
  United Methodist Church

Ed Doty
  Youth Service Opportunities Project

Ernestine Galloway
  American Bible Society

Dorothy Gist
  Episcopal Church Center

Kate Haser
  Jesuit Volunteer Corps: East

Linda Crawford Hodges
  Presbyterian Church (U.S.A.)

Donald D. Jackson
  Evangelical Lutheran Church in America

Nancy Kleppel
  Maryknoll Fathers and Brothers

Kristen Mayhue
  Mennonite Voluntary Service

Jayna Powell
  Christian Church

Jack Reentz
  Evangelical Lutheran Church in America

Jim Reid
  International Christian Youth Exchange

Mike Robertson
  Southern Baptist Convention

Bill Rollins
  United Methodist Church

Susan Sanders
  United Church Board for Homeland Ministries

Janet Schrock
  Brethren Volunteer Service

Michael Stuart
  Presbyterian Church (U.S.A.)

Lee W. Tyler
  Diaconal Ministry

L. William Yolton
  NISBCO

P. Bart York
  Habitat for Humanity

Paul Yount
  National Council of Churches

For further information, write to CRVA, 475 Riverside Drive, Room 668, New York, NY 10115; (212) 870-2368.

Appendix II
Council on International Educational Exchange (CIEE)

The Council on International Educational Exchange (CIEE) is a private, nonprofit organization with offices in the U.S., Europe, and Asia. In its 45 years of service to the educational community, CIEE has emerged as one of the foremost organizations promoting international education and student travel.

CIEE was founded in 1947 to help reestablish student exchanges after World War II. In its early years, the council chartered ocean liners for transatlantic student sailings, arranged group air travel, and organized orientation programs to prepare students and teachers for educational experiences abroad. Over the years, CIEE's mandate has broadened dramatically as the interests of its ever-increasing membership have spread beyond Europe to Africa, Asia, and Latin America. Today, CIEE assumes a number of important responsibilities that include developing and administering programs of international educational exchange throughout the world, coordinating work-abroad programs as well as international workcamps, and facilitating inexpensive international travel for students, teachers, and other budget travelers.

Study Abroad

In cooperation with a number of North American colleges and universities, CIEE's University Programs Department administers study-abroad programs for college and university students in Argentina, Australia, Brazil, Chile, China, Costa Rica, Czechoslovakia, the Dominican Republic, France, Germany, Hungary, Indonesia, Japan, Poland, Russia, Spain, Thailand, and Vietnam. Designed for undergraduates and graduates alike, the programs are open to qualified students.

Work Abroad

CIEE's Work Exchanges Department operates a series of work-abroad programs that allow U.S. students to obtain temporary employment in Britain, Canada, Costa Rica, Czechoslovakia, France, Germany, Ireland, Jamaica, New Zealand, and Spain. These programs enable students to avoid the red tape and bureaucratic difficulties that usually accompany the process of getting permission to work in a foreign country. Along with the necessary employment authorization, work-abroad participants receive general information on the country, tips on employment, and helpful hints on housing and travel. In each country the program is offered in cooperation with a national student organization or CIEE office that provides and orientation on the country's culture and society, advises on seeking jobs and accommodations, and serves as a sponsor during the participant's stay.

International Voluntary Service

CIEE's Voluntary Service Department operates an international workcamp program for young people interested in short-term voluntary service overseas. More information on this program is available on page 55 of this book.

High School Programs

CIEE's Secondary Education Programs Department administers School Partners Abroad, which matches junior and senior high schools in the U.S. with counterpart schools in Europe, Asia, and Latin America. The program involves participating schools in an array of year-round curriculum-related activities, the centerpiece of which is an annual exchange of students and teachers. Also available to U.S. high school students is Youth in China, a unique summer study program in Xi'an, China.

Adult/Professional Programs

The Professional and Continuing Education Programs Department designs and administers a wide variety of short-term seminars and in-service training programs for groups of international professionals, including secondary-school teachers and administrators, university faculty, business managers, and other "adult learners." Among these programs is the International Faculty Develpment Seminar series, for faculty and administrators at two- and four- year institutions of higher education. These overseas seminars and professional interchange opportunities are designed to assist institutions with internationalizing home-campus curricula.

Student Services

Through its Information and Student Services Department, CIEE sponsors the International Student Identity Card in the United States. Nearly 200,000 cards are issued each year by CIEE's New York headquarters, its 36 Council Travel offices and more than 450 issuing offices at colleges and universities across the country. Cardholders receive travel-related discounts, basic accident/medical insurance coverage while traveling abroad, and access to a 24-hour toll-free emergency hotline. Also sponsored by CIEE are the International Youth Identity Card for those under 26, and the International Teacher Identity Card for full-time faculty—

both of which provide benefits similar to the International Student Identity Card. The department also administers the International Student Identity Card Fund. Supported by the sale of the International Student Identity Card in the United States, the fund offers travel grants to U.S. high school and undergraduate students participating in study or service programs in the Third World countries of Africa, Asia, and Latin America.

Publications

CIEE's *Student Travel Catalog* is a free 76-page brochure that is read by hundreds of thousands of people each year. The *Catalog* contains all kinds of useful information for anyone considering a trip abroad, as well as forms that can be used to order CIEE publications and apply for CIEE programs.

In addition to *Volunteer!*, CIEE publishes the following books:
- *Work, Study, Travel Abroad: The Whole World Handbook*, edited by Del Franz and published by St. Martin's Press. This guide introduces all the essentials of working, studying, and traveling abroad, and covers the map of available choices and options in 75 countries on six continents. It shows the traveler how to experience another country as an insider.
- *The Teenager's Guide to Study, Travel, and Adventure Abroad*, compiled by CIEE and published by St. Martin's Press, is an award-winning compendium of short- and long-term overseas opportunities for youths 12 to 18 years of age.
- *Where to Stay USA*, is a state-by-state listing of more than 1,700 places to spend the night for under $30, with special city sections and general travel advice for anyone touring the United States; updated every other year by CIEE and published by Prentice Hall.

Charter Flights

Council Charter, a subsidiary of CIEE, offers budget flights between the U.S. and Europe on scheduled and charter carriers that are open to students and nonstudents alike. Cities served vary slightly each year; in 1991 flights were available to Amsterdam, Brussels, London, Lyons, Madrid, Málaga, Milan, Nice, Paris, and Rome. Council Charter allows you to fly to one city and return from another, and offers a low-cost cancellation waiver which allows you to cancel your flight as late as three hours before departure with no penalty.

Travel Services

Council Travel operates a network of 36 retail travel offices across the country that provide travel assistance to students, teachers, and other budget travelers planning individual or group trips to any part of the world. Council Travel services and products include:

- low-cost flights between the U.S. and Europe, Asia, the South Pacific, Africa, the Middle East, Latin America, and the Caribbean on scheduled and charter carriers; many of these fares are available only to students or young people
- rail passes, including Eurail, BritRail, and French Rail passes
- the International Student Identity Card, the International Youth Identity Card, and the International Teacher Identity Card
- car-rental plans in Europe
- language courses in 17 European cities and Japan
- travel insurance, guidebooks, and travel gear

Following is a list of Council Travel office locations and telephone numbers in the United States:

Amherst, MA
(413) 256-1261

Ann Arbor, MI
(313) 998-0200

Atlanta, GA
(404) 377-9997

Austin, TX
(512) 472-4931

Berkeley, CA
(415) 848-8604

Boston, MA
(617) 266-1926
(617) 424-6665

Boulder, CO
(303) 447-8101

Cambridge, MA
(617) 497-1497
(617) 225-2555

Chicago, IL
(312) 951-0585

Columbus, OH
(614) 294-8696

Dallas, TX
(214) 363-9941

Durham, NC
(919) 286-4664

Evanston, IL
(708) 475-5070

La Jolla, CA
(619) 452-0630

Long Beach, CA
(310) 598-3338
(714) 527-7950

Los Angeles, CA
(310) 208-3551

Milwaukee, WI
(414) 332-4740

Minneapolis, MN
(612) 379-2323

New Haven, CT
(203) 562-5335

New Orleans, LA
(504) 866-1767

New York, NY
(212) 661-1450
(212) 254-2525
(212) 666-4177

Philadelphia, PA
(215) 382-0343

Portland, OR
(503) 228-1900

Providence, RI
(401) 331-5810

San Diego, CA
(619) 270-6401

San Francisco, CA
(415) 421-3473
(415) 566-6222

Seattle, WA
(206) 632-2448
(206) 329-4567

Sherman Oaks, CA
(818) 905-5777

Tempe, AZ
(602) 966-3544

Washington, DC
(202) 337-6464

CIEE Membership

At present, over 225 educational institutions and organizations in the United States and abroad are members of CIEE. As members, they may take advantage of CIEE's information and publications services; become involved in CIEE's advocacy, evaluation, and consultation activities; and participate in conferences and services organized by CIEE. Membership allows educational institutions and organizations to play a central role in the development and operation of exchanges at a national and international level. Members of the Council on International Educational Exchange are:

Adelphi University
Adventist Colleges Abroad
AFS International/Intercultural
  Programs
Albertson College of Idaho
Alma College
American Council on the
  Teaching of Foreign Languages
American Graduate School of
  International Management
American Heritage Association
American University
American University in Cairo
American Youth Hostels, Inc.
Antioch University
Arkansas College
Associated Colleges of the
  Midwest
Association for International
  Practical Training
Association of Student Councils
  (Canada)
Attila Jozsef University
Bates College
Beaver College
Beloit College
Boston College
Boston University
Bradford College
Brandeis University
Brethren Colleges Abroad
Brigham Young University

Brown University
Bucknell University
Butler University
California State University
California State University, Long
  Beach
California State University,
  Sacramento
Carleton College
Carroll College
Central Michigan University
Central University of Iowa
Central Washington University
Chapman College
College of Charleston
Colorado College
Colorado State University
Cornell University
Curtin University of Technology
Dartmouth College
Davidson College
DePauw University
Drake University
Earlham College
Eastern Michigan University
Eckerd College
École Centrale de Paris
Elmira College
Empire State College—SUNY
Experiment in International Living
Georgetown University
Gonzaga University

176 Volunteer!

Goshen College
Great Lakes Colleges Association
Grinnell College
Guilford College
Gustavus Adolphus College
Hampshire College
Hartwick College
Harvard College
Hebrew University of Jerusalem
Heidelberg College
Hiram College
Hollins College
Hope College
Illinois State University
Indiana University
Institute of International Education
International Christian University
International Christian Youth Exchange
International Student Exchange Program
Iowa State University
James Madison University
Kalamazoo College
Kent State University
Lake Erie College
Lancaster University
LaSalle University
Lehigh University
Lewis & Clark College
Lisle Fellowship, Inc.
Louisiana State University
Loyola Marymount University
Macalester College
Marquette University
Mary Baldwin College
Memphis State University
Miami University
Michigan State University
Middlebury College
Millersville State College
Monterey Institute of International Studies
Moorhead State University
Murdoch University
National Association of Secondary School Principals
New York University
North Carolina State University at Raleigh
Northeastern University
Northern Arizona University
Northern Illinois University
Northern Michigan University
Northfield Mount Hermon School
Oberlin College
Obirin University
Ohio University
Ohio State University
Open Door Student Exchange
Pace University
Pennsylvania State University
Pitzer College
Pomona College
Portland State University
Purdue University
Ramapo College of New Jersey
Reed College
Reformed Church in America
Rhode Island School of Design
Rochester Institute of Technology
Rollins College
Rosary College
Rutgers University
St. John Fisher College
St. Lawrence University
St. Olaf College
St. Peter's College
State University of New Jersey
Scandinavian Seminar
School Year Abroad
Scripps College
Skidmore College
Southern Illinois University at Carbondale
Southern Methodist University
Southwest Texas State University

Spelman College
Springfield College
Stanford University
State University of New York
Stephens College
Stetson University
Syracuse University
Texas A&M University
Texas Tech University
Trinity College
Tufts University
Tulane University
Universidad Autónoma de Guadalajara
Universidad de Belgrano
University College London
Université de Bordeaux III
University of Alabama
University of Alabama at Birmingham
University of Arkansas at Little Rock
University of British Columbia
University of California
University of Colorado at Boulder
University of Connecticut
University of Copenhagen (DIS Study)
University of Denver
University of Essex
University of Evansville
University of Hartford
University of Illinois
University of Iowa
University of Kansas
University of La Verne
University of Louisville
University of Maine at Orono
University of Maryland
University of Massachusetts
University of Michigan
University of Minnesota
University of New Hampshire
University of North Carolina at Chapel Hill
University of North Texas
University of Notre Dame
University of Oklahoma
University of Oregon
University of the Pacific
University of Pennsylvania
University of Pittsburgh
University of Rhode Island
University of St. Thomas
University of South Carolina
University of Southern California
University of Sussex
University of Tennessee
University of Texas at Austin
University of Toledo
University of Utah
University of Vermont
University of Virginia
University of Washington
University of Wisconsin—Green Bay
University of Wisconsin—Madison
University of Wisconsin—Milwaukee
University of Wisconsin—Platteville
University of Wisconsin—River Falls
University of Wollongong
University of Wyoming
University System of Georgia
Valparaiso University
Volunteers in Asia
Wake Forest University
Washington State University
Wayne State University
Wesleyan University
Western Michigan University
Western Washington University
Westminster College

Whitman College
Whitworth College
Wichita State University
Wilmington College
Wittenberg University

Wofford College
World College West
YMCA of the USA International Program Services
Youth For Understanding

Associate Members

American Center for Students and Artists
Association of College Unions—International
Canadian Bureau for International Education
European Association for International Education
Fontainebleau Fine Arts and Music Schools Association

Japan International Christian University Foundation, Inc.

NAFSA: Association of International Educators

National Association for Equal Opportunity in Higher Education (NAFEO)

United Negro College Fund

For further information, write to: CIEE, 205 East 42nd Street, New York, NY 10017; (212) 661-1414.

INDEX

Organizations

ACTION, 8, 162
Alabama Council on Human Relations, 103
Alderson Hospitality House, 103
All-Union Student Brigade, 41
American Farm School/Summer Work Activities Program, 41
American Friends Service Committee, 41
American Hiking Society, 42
American Jewish Society for Service, 43
American Red Cross, 19
American Refugee Committee, 10, 103
Amigos de las Americas, 43
Andover Foundation for Archaeological Research, 44
Année Diaconale, 104
Annunciation House, 44, 104
Appalachian Trail Conference, 45
Archaeological Institute of America, 6
Archaeology Abroad, 6
Architects and Planners in Support of Nicaragua, 46
Association Culturelle des Activités d'Amitié et d'Echange entre Jeunes, 46
Association of Episcopal Colleges, 105
Association of Volunteers for Service in Protected Areas, 47
Association Tunisienne d'Action Volontaire, 47
Australian Trust for Conservation Volunteers, 48
Bangladesh Work Camps Association, 48

Boys Hope, 48, 106
Brethren Volunteer Service, 106
Brother Benno Foundation, 108
Camphill Village Trust, 108
Campus Outreach Opportunity League, 18
Canadian Bureau for International Education, 49
Caribbean Conservation Corporation, 49
Caritas Mission, 108
Carrefour Canadien International, 50
Casa Juan Diego, 109
Casa Ricardo Chacon, 110
Catholic Medical Mission Board, 50, 110
Catholic Volunteers in Florida, 111
Cecil Houses, 111
Centre for Youth and Social Development, 51
Centro Adelante Campesino, 112
Chantiers Jeunesse Maroc, 51
Cheyenne River Youth Project, 112
Christian Appalachian Project, 113
Christian Foundation on Children and Aging, 113
Christian Welfare and Social Relief, 52
Church World Service, 114
City Volunteer Corps, 114
CKM/KMC, 52
Club de Vieux Manoir, 53

Club UNESCO "Martin Luther King," 116
Coalition for the Homeless, 10, 116
Colorado Trail Foundation, 53
Community for Creative Non-Violence, 116
Community Service Volunteers, 117
Compagnons Bâtisseurs, 54
Concern/America, 117
Concordia, 54
Coordinating Committee for International Voluntary Service, 19
Council of Religious Volunteer Agencies, vii
Council on International Educational Exchange, vii, 5, 21, 46, 47, 49, 51, 52, 54, 55, 62, 71, 72, 73, 79, 93, 95, 96, 97, 99
Council Travel, 175–176
Covenant House, 118
Cross-Lines Cooperative Council, 119
Crow Canyon Archaeological Center, 56
CUSO, 119
Daughters of Charity—Associates in Mission, 120
Dental Health International, 10, 121
Diaconal Ministry, 121
Diocesan Lay Volunteer Program—Diocese of Salt Lake City, 122
Dooley Foundation—Intermed USA, 123
Dorset Natural History and Archaeological Society, 56
Earthstewards Network, 56
Earthwatch, 6, 57
East Coast Migrant Health Project, 123

Eclaireuses et Eclaireurs du Senegal, 57
Ecumenical Young Adult Ministry Staff Team, 58
EIRENE, 124
Episcopal Church Volunteers for Mission, 124
Esperança, 58
Ethnic and Cultural Practicum, 59
The Experiment in International Living, 59
Focus, 60
Food for the Hungry, 125
Foundation for Field Research, 6, 61
Foundation for International Youth Exchange, 62
Four Corners School of Outdoor Education, 62
Fourth World Movement, 10, 63, 126
Franciscan Outreach Association, 127
Friends of the Third World, 127
Friends Weekend Workcamps, 63
Frontiers Foundation/Operation Beaver, 64
Genctur Tourism and Travel, 64
Genesis II, 65
Global Volunteers, 66
Gruppo Volontari della Svizzera Italiana, 66
Habitat for Humanity, 128
Health Volunteers Overseas, 10, 129
Heifer Project International Learning and Livestock Center, 66
Helen Keller International, 130
Human Environment Center, 18
Human Service Alliance, 67, 130
Innisfree, 131
Institute of Cultural Affairs, 68
Instituto de la Juventud, 69
InterAction, 18

Index

Intercultural Press, 20
International Association of Dental Students, 69
International Christian Youth Exchange, 58, 70, 131
International Eye Foundation, 10, 132
International Liaison of Lay Volunteers in Mission, 133
International Lifeline, 133
International Rescue Committee, 10, 134
International Voluntary Service, 70
International Voluntary Services, 134
Internationale Begegnung Gemeinschaftsdiensten, 71
Internationale Jugendgemeinschaftsdienste, 71
Interns for Peace, 135
Involvement Volunteers, 72
Israel Department of Antiquities and Museums, 72
Jesuit Volunteer Corps, 136
Jeunesse et Reconstruction, 73
Joint Assistance Centre, 73
Jubilee Partners, 137
Kibbutz Aliya, 74
Koinonia Partners, 74
La Sabranenque, 76
Lalmba Association, 137
L'Arche Mobile, 75, 138
Leonard Cheshire Foundation, 138
Lisle Fellowship, 76
Los Niños, 77,
Lutheran Volunteer Corps, 138
Lutheran World Mission Volunteers, 139
Macon Program for Progress, 78
Malta Youth Hostels Association, 78
Marianist Voluntary Service Communities, 140

Maryknoll Lay Missioners, 140
Mellemfolkeligt Samvirke, 79
Mendenhall Ministries, 141
Mennonite Board of Missions, 141
Mennonite Central Committee, 79, 142
Mennonite Voluntary Service, 143
Mercy Corps, 144
Mercy Corps International, 144
Mir Initiative, 80
Mission Volunteers/USA, 144
Mobility International/USA, 80
National Association of Service and Conservation Corps, 18
National Farm Worker Ministry, 145
National Trust for Places of Natural Beauty and Historic Interest, 81
National Venceremos Brigade, 81
Nothelfergemeinschaft Der Freunde, 82
The Ockenden Venture, 146
Open Door Community, 146
Operation Crossroads Africa, 82
Overseas Development Network, 83, 147
Partners of the Americas, 84
Partnership for Service Learning, 10, 84, 147
Peace Corps, 8, 21, 148
Peace Village International, 149
Plenty International, 85
Ponape Agriculture and Trade School, 149

Project Concern International/Options Service, 86, 150
Project Hope, 150
Project ORBIS, 86
Queen Elizabeth's Foundation for the Disabled, 87
Queen Louise Home for Children, 151
R.E.M.P. ART., 88
The Richmond Fellowship International, 151
Royal Society for Mentally Handi-capped Children and Adults, 88
St. Joseph's Indian School, 152
Service Archéologique du Musée de Douai, 89
Service Civil International—International Voluntary Service, 5, 70, 89, 96, 97,
The Shaftesbury Society, 152
Sherut La'am, 153
Simon Community, 154
Sioux Indian YMCAs, 90
SIW Internationale Vrijwilligerprojekten, 90
SMA Lay Missionaries, 155
Stella Maris School of Nursing, 155
Student Conservation Association, 91
Tallahatchie Development League, 92, 156
UNAREC, 92
United Church Board for Homeland Ministries, 156
United Methodist Volunteers in Mission, 157
United Nations Association, 93
United Nations Volunteer Program, 8, 158
United States Forest Service
  Alaska Region, 93, 159
  Northern Region, 94, 159
  Pacific Northwest Region, 94, 160
Vereinigung Junger Freiwilliger, 95
Vincentian Service Corps, 160
Visions in Action, 160
VISTA, 8, 161
Voluntarios Internacionales México, 95
Voluntary Service Slovenia, 96
Voluntary Workcamps Association of Ghana, 97
Voluntary Workcamps Association of Nigeria, 97
Volunteer Optometric Service to Humanity, 96
Volunteers for Educational and Social Services, 161
Volunteers for Peace, 5, 49, 51, 52, 72, 73, 79, 93, 95, 96, 97, 98
Volunteers in Asia, 20
Volunteers in Technical Assistance, 162
Winant-Clayton Volunteers, 99
Workcamps Office of DEMISZ, 99
World Assembly of Youth, 162
World Council of Churches, 163
WorldTeach, 10, 163
World Vision, 164
The WUJS Institute, 165
Wycliffe Bible Translators, 165
YMCA of the USA, 10, 166
YMCA International Camp Counselor Program, 100
Youth Service Opportunities Project, 100

Skills Needed

Advocacy, 80, 136, 142, 143, 145, 146

Agriculture, 41, 50, 52, 58, 59, 67, 74, 77, 81, 84, 85, 95, 98, 120, 124, 125, 135, 139, 141, 142, 144, 148, 149, 155, 158, 163, 164

Archaeology, 6, 44, 52, 55, 56, 57, 61, 62, 69, 72, 89, 93, 98, 159

Arts, 42, 84, 100, 112

Business/technical consulting, 46, 50, 66, 84, 85, 110, 111, 120, 124, 125, 135, 137, 139, 142, 148, 155, 158, 163, 164, 165

Camp counseling, 49, 51, 90, 100

Childcare, 42, 58, 64, 100, 103, 111, 112, 113, 114, 121, 126, 128, 136, 139, 143, 145, 151, 160

Clerical, 58, 63, 67, 73, 75, 78, 92, 94, 106, 110, 112, 125, 126, 127, 128, 137, 141, 143, 147, 155, 156, 158, 159, 163

Community service outreach, 41, 45, 49, 50, 51, 59, 63, 64, 66, 67, 68, 70, 72, 73, 75, 77, 78, 79, 80, 82, 84, 85, 87, 88, 90, 92, 93, 97, 99, 100, 103, 104, 105, 106, 108, 109, 111, 112, 113, 114, 116, 117, 118, 126, 127, 130, 131, 132, 135, 136, 138, 139, 140, 141, 142, 143, 145, 146, 148, 149, 151, 151, 153, 154, 156, 158, 160, 161

   Service to the disabled, 64, 67, 75, 80, 82, 87, 88, 93, 99, 104, 105, 108, 111, 117, 130, 131, 132, 138, 140, 153, 156

   Service to the homeless, 45, 99, 100, 104, 105, 106, 108, 111, 116, 117, 127, 139, 140, 146, 154

   Service to the young, 45, 47, 49, 64, 77, 78, 90, 93, 99, 104, 105, 106, 112, 113, 114, 117, 118, 132, 136, 140, 141, 143, 145, 149, 151, 156, 161

   Service to the aged, 64, 78, 82, 104, 106, 109, 111, 112, 113, 114, 117, 132, 136, 139, 140, 143, 156, 161

   Service to the mentally ill, 117, 151

   Service to women, 111, 132, 136, 143

Computer skills, 46, 121, 128, 139, 147, 153

Conservation, 46, 47, 48, 50, 52, 54, 55, 56, 57, 58, 59, 60, 62, 65, 69, 70, 71, 72, 73, 79, 80, 81, 85, 90, 91, 93, 94, 95, 96, 98, 99, 132, 153, 159, 160

Construction/building maintenance, 42, 43, 45, 46, 47, 48, 49, 51, 52, 53, 54, 55, 58, 59, 62, 63, 64, 65, 66, 67, 69, 70, 72, 73, 74, 75, 78, 79, 80, 81, 82, 92, 96, 97, 103, 104, 106, 109, 113, 114, 119, 125, 126, 128, 137, 139, 141, 142, 143, 144, 148, 149, 155, 156, 158, 163

Cycling, 83

Dentistry, 69, 110, 121, 129

Education, 46, 47, 49, 50, 51, 52, 58, 59, 62, 63, 66, 72, 77, 81, 84, 85, 90, 92, 103, 105, 106, 109, 110, 111, 112, 113, 114, 116, 118, 119, 120, 121, 125, 126, 134, 136, 137, 140, 141, 142, 143, 145, 148, 149,

151, 152, 153, 155, 156, 158, 159, 160, 161, 163, 166
Engineering, 46, 104, 125, 148, 158
Farming/gardening, 41, 42, 63, 67, 75, 79, 81, 85, 112, 137, 141
Forestry, 46, 47, 48, 57, 65, 91, 94, 120, 125, 148, 159, 160
Health care, 44, 45, 48, 50, 58, 66, 67, 70, 77, 84, 85, 86, 103, 104, 105, 106, 110, 113, 118, 121, 122, 123, 124, 125, 129, 130, 133, 135, 139, 140, 141, 142, 143, 144, 145, 148, 149, 150, 151, 153, 155, 160, 164, 165
Journalism, 125, 160
Language ability in,
 Arabic, 135
 Creole, 124
 French, 50, 54, 58, 66, 89, 92, 104, 105, 116, 124, 135, 139, 145, 163
 German, 71, 95, 145, 149
 Hebrew, 135, 154
 Italian, 66
 Khmer, 104
 Portuguese, 59
 Russian, 80
 Spanish, 42, 45, 46, 47, 59, 69, 77, 95, 103, 104, 105, 109, 110, 111, 113, 119, 124, 135, 139, 142, 143, 145, 151, 163
 Wolof, 116
Legal/paralegal, 92, 118, 136, 141, 143, 156
Manual labor, 41, 42, 43, 44, 45, 46, 47, 48, 49, 51, 52, 53, 54, 55, 56, 57, 58, 59, 61, 62, 63, 64, 65, 66, 67, 69, 71, 72, 73, 74, 76, 78, 79, 80, 81, 82, 83, 85, 88, 89, 90, 91, 92, 93, 94, 95, 96, 97, 98, 99, 108, 113, 114, 119, 125, 126, 128, 137, 141, 142, 143, 148, 155, 156, 163
Mechanics, 41, 46, 75, 139, 149, 165

Medicine, 50, 86, 104, 110, 114, 118, 123, 128, 130, 133, 137, 144, 145, 150, 151, 155, 165
Midwifery, 104
Ministry/religious services, 59, 111, 113, 119, 121, 122, 124, 136, 141, 142, 143, 144, 145, 146, 155, 156, 161
No special skills required, 41, 43, 46, 47, 48, 49, 50, 51, 52, 53, 54, 55, 56, 57, 58, 59, 61, 62, 63, 64, 65, 66, 67, 68, 70, 71, 72, 73, 74, 75, 76, 77, 78, 79, 80, 81, 82, 83, 85, 87, 88, 89, 90, 91, 92, 93, 94, 95, 96, 97, 98, 99, 100, 103, 104, 105, 108, 109, 111, 112, 113, 114, 116, 117, 119, 124, 125, 126, 127, 128, 130, 131, 132, 137, 139, 140, 141, 142, 143, 145, 146, 148, 155, 156, 160, 163
Nursing, 50, 59, 86, 104, 110, 111, 123, 128, 130, 133, 136, 137, 140, 145, 150, 152, 155, 161, 165
Nutrition, 77, 92, 123, 130, 143, 156
Ophthalmology, 59, 60, 86, 96, 130, 132
Opticians, 86, 96
Optometrists, 86, 96
Orthopedics, 59, 128
Outdoor skills, 42, 45, 53, 62, 65
Park maintenance/trailbuiding, 42, 45, 52, 53, 55, 57, 70, 71, 80, 91, 92, 94, 99, 114, 159, 160
Plastic surgery, 59
Physical therapy, 123, 128, 136, 153
Psychiatry, 104,
Recreation, 49, 66, 71, 84, 90, 92, 93, 100, 109, 112, 119, 136, 144, 156, 163
Refugee work, 45, 60, 90, 103, 104, 106, 110, 114, 117, 134, 137, 143, 146
Research, 68, 72, 123, 126, 127, 160

Respite care, 67, 130
Restoration/preservation, 41, 49, 52, 53, 54, 62, 71, 73, 76, 79, 81, 88, 92, 95, 96, 98,
Social work, 45, 49, 52, 54, 70, 71, 72, 73, 85, 96, 98, 103, 104, 106, 109, 111, 112, 121, 123, 124, 142, 143, 144, 148, 152, 153, 160, 161

Teaching/tutoring, 49, 51, 52, 58, 59, 66, 73, 77, 84, 85, 90, 92, 94, 103, 105, 106, 109, 110, 111, 112, 113, 114, 116, 117, 118, 119, 120, 124, 134, 136, 137, 140, 141, 143, 144, 145, 148, 149, 152, 153, 155, 156, 158, 159, 160, 161, 163, 165, 166
Translation, 165

Location of Programs

Africa, 47, 50, 51, 52, 55, 57, 58, 60, 61, 66, 69, 70, 82, 83, 84, 85, 86, 96, 97, 98, 100, 105, 110, 113, 116, 117, 120, 121, 123, 124, 128, 132, 133, 135, 137, 139, 141, 148, 150, 155, 158, 160, 163
Alabama, 75, 103, 138
Alaska, 93, 159
Algeria, 55
Angola, 13
Appalachia, 79, 113
Arizona, 49, 61, 62, 106, 112, 127, 142
Arkansas, 67
Asia, 41, 48, 50, 57, 58, 60, 66, 70, 72, 73, 74, 77, 80, 84, 85, 86, 96, 100, 105, 110, 113, 120, 121, 128, 132, 134, 135, 139, 141, 148, 150, 158, 160, 163, 166
Australia, 48, 60, 72, 100, 132
Bali, 60, 77
Bangladesh, 48, 128, 135
Belgium, 54, 55, 63, 68, 104, 124
Belize, 85
Bhutan, 121, 128
Bolivia, 84, 113, 135, 140
Botswana, 83,
Brazil, 44, 59, 60, 113, 141
Bulgaria, 55

California, 49, 61, 72, 103, 108, 119, 127, 142, 145, 147
Cambodia, 103
Cameroon, 121, 139
Canada, 49, 50, 55, 57, 64, 79, 91, 119, 128
Caribbean, 42, 44, 50, 61, 66, 82, 83, 84, 85, 105, 110, 113, 120, 129, 132, 148, 151, 158
Chad, 124
Chile, 113, 141
China, 128, 163
Colombia, 113
Colorado, 53, 56, 62, 79, 142
Connecticut, 61
Cook Islands, 121
Costa Rica, 44, 47, 50, 57, 65, 113, 163
Côte d'Ivoire, 83
Cuba, 42, 81
Czechoslovakia, 52, 55
Delaware, 139
Denmark, 55, 79, 163
Dominican Republic, 44, 84, 85, 113
Ecuador, 44, 60, 84, 105, 135, 148,
Egypt, 129
El Salvador, 113, 117

England, 56, 60, 63, 81, 84, 87, 88, 99, 105, 111, 117, 138, 146, 148, 152, 153, 154
Ethiopia, 129
Europe, 41, 46, 52, 53, 54, 55, 56, 57, 60, 61, 62, 63, 65, 66, 68, 69, 70, 71, 72, 73, 76, 78, 79, 81, 82, 84, 85, 87, 88, 89, 90, 92, 95, 96, 98, 99, 100, 104, 105, 111, 117, 124, 132, 138, 146, 148, 149, 150, 152, 153, 154, 158, 163
Faroe Islands, 79
Fiji, 72
Florida, 42, 111, 119, 123, 145
France, 46, 53, 54, 55, 60, 61, 70, 73, 76, 84, 88, 89, 92, 105, 124, 148
Gambia, 83
Georgia, 75, 123, 137, 146
Germany, 55, 60, 61, 63, 71, 72, 82, 95, 132, 149
Ghana, 55, 61, 70, 83, 97
Greenland, 79
Grenada, 61, 129
Greece, 41
Guatemala, 66, 68, 113, 141
Haiti, 113
Hawaii, 42, 91
Honduras, 66, 113, 117
Hong Kong, 141
Hungary, 55, 99
Iceland,
Idaho, 94, 159
Illinois, 43, 49, 68, 103, 106, 121, 139, 142, 145
India, 50, 51, 72, 73, 77, 84, 85, 86, 105, 110, 113, 129, 148, 160
Indiana, 121, 127
Indonesia, 60, 66, 129
Ireland, 55, 60, 124
Israel, 73, 74, 135, 141, 153, 165
Italy, 60, 61
Jamaica, 66, 84, 105, 129, 148
Japan, 60, 77, 132, 141, 166

Kansas, 43, 119
Kentucky, 113, 140
Kenya, 60, 83, 86, 113, 137, 141, 160
Korea, 141
Latin America, 42, 44, 45, 46, 47, 50, 57, 58, 59, 60, 61, 65, 66, 68, 70, 77, 81, 84, 85, 86, 91, 95, 96, 98, 100, 104, 105, 110, 113, 120, 123, 124, 132, 135, 141, 148, 150, 155, 158, 163
Lesotho, 83
Liberia, 61, 84, 105, 139, 148
Louisiana, 49, 106, 119, 121
Madagascar, 113, 139
Maine, 123
Malawi, 103, 129
Malta, 78
Maryland, 123, 139, 142
Mexico, 42, 44, 45, 57, 60, 61, 66, 68, 77, 84, 91, 95, 104, 105, 113, 117, 129, 132, 148, 155
Michigan, 49, 106, 121, 145
Micronesia, 148, 149
Middle East, 72, 129, 135, 141, 153, 163, 165
Minnesota, 103, 139
Mississippi, 66, 92, 141, 142, 156
Missouri, 49, 106, 121, 122
Montana, 61, 159
Morocco, 51, 55
Mozambique, 129, 13
Namibia, 163
Nepal, 86, 139
Netherlands, 55, 63, 90,
New Jersey, 123
New Mexico, 62
New York, 49, 61, 68, 100, 106, 114, 119, 123, 140, 142, 145
New Zealand, 132
Nicaragua, 46, 57, 113, 124, 141
Niger, 124
Nigeria, 60, 97,
North America, 42, 43, 44, 45, 49, 53, 55, 56, 57, 59, 61, 62, 63, 64,

66, 67, 68, 75, 77, 78, 79, 83, 84, 90, 91, 92, 93, 94, 100, 103, 104, 105, 106, 108, 109, 110, 111, 112, 113, 114, 116, 119, 121, 122, 123, 124, 127, 128, 130, 131, 136, 137, 138, 139, 140, 141, 142, 143, 144, 145, 146, 147, 148, 150, 152, 156, 158, 159, 160, 161
North Carolina, 67, 78, 123, 130
North Dakota, 94, 159
Northern Ireland, 70
Oceania, 50, 57, 66, 72, 100, 110, 120, 121, 132, 139, 149
Ohio, 49, 77, 106, 140, 145
Oregon, 57, 61, 94, 160
Pakistan, 129, 134
Panama, 57
Papua New Guinea, 139
Paraguay, 44
Pennsylvania, 49, 63, 106, 108, 123, 142
Peru, 68, 113
Philippines, 84, 105, 113, 148
Poland, 55, 62, 66, 163
Polynesia, 148
Russia, 41, 55, 60, 80, 91
Rwanda, 121, 133
St. Kitts, 113
St. Lucia, 129
St. Vincent, 60, 84
Scotland, 84, 108, 148,
Senegal, 58, 83, 116
Sierra Leone, 52, 61, 117
South Africa, 160, 163
South Carolina, 123
South Dakota, 84, 90, 94, 105, 112, 148, 152, 159
South Pacific, 57, 66, 72, 120, 121, 149
Soviet Union (former), 41, 55, 60, 80, 91, 98
Spain, 55, 60, 61, 69
Sudan, 137
Switzerland, 60, 63, 66, 71, 124

Taiwan, 141, 166
Tanzania, 66, 83, 139, 141
Tennessee, 123
Texas, 45, 104, 109, 110, 119, 121, 127, 142, 145, 161
Thailand, 60, 72, 103, 121, 141, 163
Togo, 66, 133,
Tonga, 148
Transkei, 129
Trinidad, 129
Tunisia, 47, 55
Turkey, 55, 65, 98
Uganda, 86, 129, 160
United Kingdom, 55, 56, 60, 63, 70, 81, 84, 87, 88, 93, 99, 105, 108, 111, 117, 138, 146, 148, 153, 154
United States, 42, 43, 44, 45, 49, 53, 55, 56, 57, 59, 61, 62, 63, 67, 68, 75, 77, 78, 79, 83, 84, 90, 91, 92, 93, 94, 100, 103, 104, 105, 108, 109, 110, 111, 112, 113, 114, 116, 119, 121, 122, 123, 124, 127, 128, 130, 131, 136, 137, 138, 139, 140, 131, 137, 139, 140, 142, 143, 144, 145, 146, 147, 148, 152, 156, 159, 160, 161
U.S. Virgin Islands, 42, 91, 151
Utah, 62, 122
Venezuela, 113, 141
Virginia, 131, 142
Wales, 55, 93
Washington, 43, 57, 94, 160
Washington, D.C., 116, 139, 142
West Virginia, 103
Western Samoa, 148
Wisconsin, 139
Yugoslavia, 96
Zambia, 83
Zimbabwe, 135, 139, 160

LIBRARY USE ONLY
DOES NOT CIRCULATE